PRENTICE HALL **WRITER'S SOLUTION**

Grammar Practice Book

SILVER

PRENTICE HALL
Upper Saddle River, New Jersey
Needham, Massachusetts

ISBN 0-13-434641-6

1 2 3 4 5 6 7 8 9 10   01 00 99 98 97

PRENTICE HALL
Simon & Schuster Education Group
A VIACOM COMPANY

Contents

1.1 Nouns

● **People, Places, and Things**

A noun is the name of a person, place, or thing.

People	Places	Things
carpenter	auditorium	*Those You Can See*
students	Grant's Tomb	hedgehog marigold
cheerleader	art gallery	ambulance blouse
Dr. Nelson	fish markets	*Those You Cannot See*
technician	Lincoln Center	warmth generosity
Canadians	Wrigley Building	sickness noise

EXERCISE A: Recognizing People, Places, and Things. Put the words below in the proper columns.

EXAMPLE: shoes (in the *Things* column)

dictionary	Stephanie	garage	umbrella	health
witness	mall	meadow	Eisenhower	envelope
sister	helicopter	dinosaur	principal	Babe Ruth
success	capitol	peanut	office	restroom

<u>People</u>   <u>Places</u>   <u>Things</u>

● **EXERCISE B: Using Nouns.** Fill in the blank in each sentence with the kind of word indicated in the parentheses.

EXAMPLE: For Christmas I got a new ___*calculator*___ .   (thing)

1. My favorite _____ will arrive from Atlanta today.   (person)

2. When will you finish your _____ ?   (thing)

3. The Supreme Court is located in _____ .   (place)

4. Until now my grandfather has always been in good _____ .   (thing)

5. You will find many reference books in the _____ .   (place)

6. Because of my poor handwriting, I need a _____ .   (thing)

7. Her _____ is appreciated by everyone.   (thing)

8. My _____ makes the best chocolate cake.   (person)

9. I always buy new records at _____ .   (place)

10. I believe the most important scientist was _____ .   (person)

1.1 Nouns

Collective Nouns

A collective noun is a noun that names a group of individual people or things.

COLLECTIVE NOUNS		
squad	flock	crew
company	team	orchard

Compound Nouns

A compound noun is made up of two or more words.

COMPOUND NOUNS	
workshop	golden rule
ice age	father-in-law

EXERCISE A: Recognizing Collective Nouns. In each blank below, write the collective noun from the sentence.

EXAMPLE: The entire clan gathered in the hall. ___clan___

1. An angry crowd assembled in front of the church. _____
2. My uncle hopes to raise a flock of sheep. _____
3. Our class voted to have a spring picnic. _____
4. Melissa applauded the performance of the orchestra. _____
5. What did you think about the reaction of the audience? _____
6. A company of dancers will entertain us first. _____
7. The jury voted to acquit the defendant. _____
8. Later, the trio played three interesting numbers. _____
9. A squadron of soldiers surrounded the building. _____
10. The bill was sent to a committee for further study. _____

EXERCISE B: Recognizing Compound Nouns. In each blank below, write the compound noun from the sentence.

EXAMPLE: We definitely need a new football. ___football___

1. My father wants to build new bookshelves. _____
2. Visit the Smithsonian Institution in Washington. _____
3. How late is the post office open on Saturday? _____
4. Her outlook is always positive. _____
5. How did your cousin like her new junior high school? _____
6. Paul Simon is my favorite songwriter. _____
7. To improve, we will need a lot of teamwork. _____
8. No medicine is a complete cure-all. _____
9. This cartridge uses an advanced magnetic tape. _____
10. We are going to assemble a new mailing list. _____

1.1 Nouns

Common and Proper Nouns

A common noun names any one of a class of people, places, or things. A proper noun names a specific person, place, or thing.

Common Nouns	Proper Nouns
soldier	General Eisenhower
theater	Globe Theater
opera	*Porgy and Bess*

EXERCISE A: Recognizing Common and Proper Nouns. In the sentences below, underline each proper noun and circle each common noun.

EXAMPLE: Bruce Springsteen is an outstanding performer.

1. Charles Dickens is easily my favorite British author.
2. The touring cast of *South Pacific* arrived early.
3. Did you know that Robert F. Kennedy once served as attorney general?
4. My math teacher at Edward R. Murrow High School is very interesting.
5. Recently, Thanksgiving was voted the most popular holiday.
6. Long ago, Rome was the largest city.
7. The library on Weldon Lane will be closed tomorrow.
8. Euripides, the tragic poet, was born in 485 B.C.
9. Andrew Carnegie built a very elaborate mansion.
10. Joe Montana is a peerless quarterback.

EXERCISE B: Changing Common Nouns into Proper Nouns. In the spaces provided below, supply a proper noun that illustrates the common noun.

EXAMPLE: a famous highway _____Pennsylvania Turnpike_____

Common Noun	Proper Noun
1. A favorite book	_____
2. A former president	_____
3. A noted composer	_____
4. A baseball team	_____
5. A beautiful river	_____
6. A famous actor	_____
7. A news magazine	_____
8. A senator	_____
9. An exciting museum	_____
10. A famous bridge	_____

1.2 | Pronouns

Antecedents of Pronouns

A pronoun is a word that takes the place of a noun. The noun it substitutes for is called an antecedent.

> **PRONOUNS AND ANTECEDENTS**
>
> ANTECEDENT PRONOUN   PRONOUN
> *Bill* raised *his* trophy in triumph and *he* smiled.
>
> PRONOUN   ANTECEDENT   PRONOUN
> Waving *her* hand, the *actress* greeted *her* fans.

Personal Pronouns

Personal pronouns refer to (1) the person speaking, (2) the person spoken to, or (3) the person, place, or thing spoken about.

First Person	Second Person	Third Person
I, me, my, mine we, us, our, ours	you, your, yours	he, him, his, she, her, hers, it, its, they, them, their, theirs

EXERCISE A: Recognizing Pronouns and Antecedents. Underline the personal pronoun in each sentence. Then circle its antecedent.

EXAMPLE: The (players) brought their lunches to the game.

1. Because of her illness, the singer was unable to appear.
2. At the party, Bob asked his sister for a dance.
3. When Betsy read *Romeo and Juliet* the first time, she cried.
4. With their tickets in hand, the three sisters approached the gangplank.
5. Jean, will you read this poem aloud?
6. In spite of their accident, the actors arrived on time.
7. The lion snarled, opened its mouth, and roared.
8. Beethoven wrote his famous *Ninth Symphony* when totally deaf.
9. Grabbing his knee, the tackle collapsed on the grass.
10. Had she wanted, Sylvia could have won the first prize.

EXERCISE B: Using Personal Pronouns in Sentences. Fill in each blank with an appropriate personal pronoun.

EXAMPLE: Of all ___*his*___ operas, Verdi liked *Macbeth* the best.

1. Susan called _____ mother as soon as dancing class was over.
2. Without _____ helmets, the football team could not play.
3. Shakespeare returned to _____ home in Stratford often.
4. These flowers are so beautiful I wish _____ would bloom all year.
5. The wingspan of the frigate bird is the largest in proportion to _____ body.
6. Were you able to get _____ autographs?
7. I want you to ask for _____ passports now.
8. Marie and _____ volunteered to work in _____ spare time.
9. Have you prepared _____ welcoming speech yet?
10. I don't think I can take _____ coin collection with us.

1.3 Four Special Kinds of Pronouns

Demonstrative Pronouns

A demonstrative pronoun points out a specific person, place, or thing. There are four demonstrative pronouns, two singular and two plural.

DEMONSTRATIVE PRONOUNS	
Singular	Plural
this	these
that	those

Relative Pronouns

A relative pronoun begins a subordinate clause and connects it to another idea in the same sentence. There are five relative pronouns.

RELATIVE PRONOUNS
that   who   whose   which   whom

EXERCISE A: Recognizing Demonstrative and Relative Pronouns. Circle the demonstrative or relative pronoun in each sentence. At the end of the sentence use a *D* to identify the pronoun as demonstrative or an *R* to identify it as relative. Note that the pronoun *that*, depending on use, can be either type.

EXAMPLE: (This) article is not correct. ___*D*___

1. Unfortunately, these are now overripe tomatoes. _____
2. Picasso is the painter whom I most admire. _____
3. Are those your books? _____
4. The book that you reserved has not yet arrived. _____
5. Is this the map of Antarctica? _____
6. The woman who is in charge just left. _____
7. That is the last piece of chicken. _____
8. Of all her photos, those are the most original in concept. _____
9. Where is the man whose dog was found? _____
10. Father decided this was the most practical van. _____

EXERCISE B: Using Demonstrative and Relative Pronouns in Sentences. Fill in each blank with an appropriate demonstrative or relative pronoun.

EXAMPLE: I wonder __*whom*__ we will meet at the dance.

1. You must walk the dog each morning. _____ is your responsibility.
2. Where is the cake _____ she chose?
3. _____ has not worked properly for some time.
4. Do you know _____ the speaker will be?
5. You really have no choice. _____ are the rules.
6. Is Mary the girl _____ grandfather is visiting?
7. Take _____ and store them in the garage.
8. Is Sandy the girl _____ he likes?
9. Give us the design _____ the manager selected.
10. The senator _____ will present the award has just arrived.

1.3 Four Special Kinds of Pronouns

Interrogative Pronouns

An interrogative pronoun is used to begin a question. There are five interrogative pronouns.

INTERROGATIVE PRONOUNS				
what	which	who	whom	whose

Indefinite Pronouns

Indefinite pronouns refer to people, places, or things, often without specifying which ones. There are many indefinite pronouns, some singular, some plural, and some either singular or plural.

INDEFINITE PRONOUNS			
Singular		**Plural**	**Singular or Plural**
anyone	neither	both	all
each	no one	few	any
either	one	many	more, most
everything	other	others	none
everyone	somebody	several	some

EXERCISE A: Recognizing Interrogative and Indefinite Pronouns. Circle the interrogative or indefinite pronoun. Identify interrogative pronouns with *int.* and indefinite pronouns with *ind.*

EXAMPLE: (No one) really knows our secret. ___*ind.*___

1. Who was chosen as our Homecoming Queen? _____
2. Both of the suggestions are extremely helpful. _____
3. Amazingly, Uncle Burt knew everyone at the dinner. _____
4. The junior prom committee accepted one of our ideas. _____
5. I found my jacket. Whose is still in the closet? _____
6. My father knows somebody at the licensing bureau. _____
7. Either of their choices is acceptable to the principal. _____
8. Have you tried some of these fabulous desserts? _____
9. Which is the shortest route to the stadium? _____
10. Many of our friends will be going on the field trip. _____

EXERCISE B: Using Interrogative and Indefinite Pronouns. Fill in each blank with an appropriate interrogative or indefinite pronoun.

EXAMPLE: I finally asked ___*someone*___ to help us.

1. _____ is the eighth-grade assistant principal?
2. The committee will examine _____ of their proposals.
3. _____ of these books are too expensive for us.
4. Can _____ enter this restricted area?
5. There are several photographs. _____ is the best?
6. Your information was wrong. _____ has to pay an entry fee.
7. _____ of the original buildings still stand on Main Street.
8. You know that _____ of H. G. Wells's predictions came true.
9. With _____ do you expect to go to the party?
10. _____ in the hall was delighted with Bill's performance.

2.1 Action Verbs

Visible and Mental Action

An action verb tells what action a person or thing is performing. Action verbs can express different kinds of actions. Some actions are visible and can easily be seen. Others are mental actions that can be seen only with difficulty, if at all.

Visible Action		Mental Action	
jump	travel	believe	pray
build	grow	know	think
jog	deliver	consider	understand

EXERCISE A: Recognizing Action Verbs. Underline the action verb in each sentence below. In the space provided, write *V* if it is a visible verb and *M* if it is a verb that indicates a mental action.

EXAMPLE: The batter <u>slid</u> into third base.   __*V*__

1. I wonder about my future almost every day. _____
2. The old locomotive pulled into the station. _____
3. Maria purchased a new wallet in the flea market. _____
4. After several hours at the beach, we drove home on the bus. _____
5. My grandmother remembers her childhood in Poland. _____
6. Some people worry almost all the time. _____
7. Cut the beef for the stew into small cubes. _____
8. This airline flies to Madrid twice weekly. _____
9. I considered my choices carefully. _____
10. After dinner, my parents opened their anniversary present. _____

EXERCISE B: Using Action Verbs in Sentences. Fill in the blanks below with appropriate action verbs. Supply the kind of action verb indicated in the parentheses.

EXAMPLE: I often __*wonder*__ about the future.   (mental)

1. A large delivery van _____ in front of our building.   (visible)
2. I often _____ about my childhood on the farm.   (mental)
3. Our committee strongly _____ in making some changes.   (mental)
4. The Independence Day Parade _____ early in the morning.   (visible)
5. Christine _____ the leading role in *West Side Story*.   (visible)
6. Our family _____ to take our vacation in August.   (mental)
7. Finally, after mother's warning, I _____ my room.   (visible)
8. I _____ exactly how to put it together.   (mental)
9. After the big snow storm, Mark _____ the driveway.   (visible)
10. Last night I _____ that I was walking down a long, dark corridor.   (mental)

2.1 Action Verbs

Transitive Verbs

An action verb is transitive if the receiver of the action is named in the sentence. The receiver of the action is called the object of the verb.

TRANSITIVE VERBS
Meg *unwrapped* her present.
(unwrapped what?) present
Mother *likes* eggs.
(likes what?) eggs

Intransitive Verbs

An action verb is intransitive if no receiver of the action is named in the sentence. A sentence with an intransitive verb will not have an object.

INTRANSITIVE VERBS
Both witnesses *agreed*.
(agreed what?) no answer
Nancy *spoke* to her doctor.
(spoke what?) no answer

EXERCISE A: Recognizing Transitive Action Verbs. Underline the transitive action verb in each sentence below and circle its object.

EXAMPLE: I have your ticket for the football game.

1. Firemen pulled the child from the burning car.
2. After a long trip we finally reached Atlanta.
3. Judy left her jacket in her school locker.
4. After dinner I enjoy a rich dessert.
5. The sergeant ordered his troops to halt.
6. Each of us named our favorite rock group.
7. Our quarterback threw a long pass for a touchdown.
8. Much to my surprise, I knew the answer to the problem.
9. Father mailed your letter in the city.
10. Carefully explain your decision to the committee.

EXERCISE B: Recognizing Intransitive Action Verbs. Underline the intransitive verb in each sentence below.

EXAMPLE: The young colt galloped alongside the fence.

1. Both my sisters sing in the church choir.
2. After listening to the charges, the manager resigned.
3. All the files burned in the fire.
4. My sister swam in the 1000-meter freestyle event.
5. The United Nations delegate flew to Geneva for a conference.
6. In Babylonian legend, Gilgamesh ruled in the kingdom of Erech.
7. The two gray cats peacefully slept on the couch.
8. Our victorious team raced off the field.
9. Receiving an enthusiastic welcome, the speaker grinned broadly.
10. The park concert lasted for almost three hours.

2.2 Linking Verbs

Forms of Be

A linking verb connects a noun or pronoun at or near the beginning of a sentence with a word at or near the end. The verb *be* is the most commonly used linking verb.

FORMS OF *BE*	
am	were being
are	can be
is	shall be
was	have been
were	should have been

Other Linking Verbs

A number of other verbs can be used as linking verbs.

OTHER LINKING VERBS		
appear	look	sound
become	remain	stay
feel	seem	taste
grow	smell	turn

EXERCISE A: Recognizing Forms of *Be* as Linking Verbs. Underline the form of *be* in each sentence below.

EXAMPLE: With luck I <u>would have been at </u>the station.

1. Hazleton is an industrial city in central Pennsylvania.
2. Who will be at the airport to greet the candidate?
3. Because of the storm, the speaker may be late.
4. My assistant will be happy to help you.
5. Until today they have been early each morning.
6. My brother is being unusually stubborn.
7. Adlai Stevenson should have been our president.
8. Your umbrella must be in the hall closet.
9. Robinson Jeffers was a fine American poet.
10. Yes, I am quite proud of my heritage.

EXERCISE B: Recognizing Other Linking Verbs. Underline the linking verb in each sentence below.

EXAMPLE: The mushroom sauce <u>tastes</u> bitter.

1. Your fundraising plan sounds excellent.
2. The president becomes a private citizen in a month.
3. The cake in the oven smells delicious.
4. The actress looked older than her pictures.
5. Grandfather feels a little better this morning.
6. This new plan seems acceptable to everyone.
7. Without refrigeration, milk quickly turns sour.
8. This new cello sounds richer than my old one.
9. After the question, the congressman appeared angry.
10. In later life my aunt grew impatient with us.

2.2 | Linking Verbs

Action Verb or Linking Verb?

To see whether a verb is a linking verb or an action verb, substitute *am*, *is* or *are* for the verb. If the sentence still makes sense and if the new verb links a word before it to a word after it, then the original verb is a linking verb.

Linking	Action
The costume *looks* interesting. (The costume *is* interesting?) linking	My brother often *looks* for his little sister. (My brother often *is* for little sister?) not linking

EXERCISE A: Distinguishing Between Action Verbs and Linking Verbs. Find and underline the verb in each sentence below. In the space provided, write *AV* for action verb or *LV* for linking verb.

EXAMPLE: At last the traveler <u>grew</u> tired. __*LV*__

1. Our neighbor remained a close friend for years. _____

2. My mother felt my head often during my illness. _____

3. Your perfume smells too strong today. _____

4. Grandmother tasted our fresh bread. _____

5. After his defeat Father felt sad for a long time. _____

6. The new snow shovel looks sturdy. _____

7. Betsy appeared troubled at her interview. _____

8. We grew two varieties of tomatoes last summer. _____

9. Your new stereo speakers sound sensational. _____

10. The bright day suddenly turned cloudy. _____

EXERCISE B: Using Action and Linking Verbs in Original Sentences. Use each verb below first as an action verb and then as a linking verb.

EXAMPLE: smell (action)   *I smell gas in the kitchen.*
       (linking)   *Our new roses smell magnificent.*

1. look   (action) _____
      (linking) _____

2. grow   (action) _____
      (linking) _____

3. feel   (action) _____
      (linking) _____

4. taste   (action) _____
      (linking) _____

5. sound   (action) _____
      (linking) _____

2.3 Helping Verbs

Recognizing Helping Verbs

Helping verbs are added before another verb to make a verb phrase. A helping verb can be one, two, or three words. Forms of the verb *be* are often used as helping verbs.

SELECTED HELPING VERBS			
is	are	was	were
has	have	had	
do	does	did	
would	should	could	
shall	will	can	may

Finding Helping Verbs in Sentences

Verb phrases are sometimes separated by such words as *not, often, slowly,* and *carefully.* In looking for helping verbs, do not include these words.

Typical Verb Phrases	Verb Phrases Separated
are growing *did* open *have been* taken *may have been* found (helping verbs in italics)	Jorge *has* certainly *been* helpful. Our friends *will* not *arrive* until evening. Dad *may have* already *started* dinner.

EXERCISE A: Recognizing Helping Verbs. In the sentences below, underline the helping verbs.

EXAMPLE: I could only <u>have</u> gone to the festival yesterday.

1. My parents have driven to Canton, Ohio, several times.
2. When are you going to the library?
3. Bill must have taken another route to the hospital.
4. She has been carefully prepared for this role.
5. My friends have often attended semipro hockey games.
6. Yes, I did explain my reasons for not going.
7. My father is not taking his vacation this year.
8. Marie could have been elected as our secretary.
9. I have carefully wrapped both lamps for shipment.
10. Can you spend a couple of hours in the park with me?

EXERCISE B: Using Helping Verbs in Sentences. Complete the sentences below by filling the blanks with appropriate helping verbs.

EXAMPLE: I ___have___ ___been___ able to find the earring.

1. We _____ _____ listening to records all day.
2. Bruce _____ not _____ reached Boston yet.
3. My mother _____ speak to the principal tomorrow.
4. I _____ _____ written my report last week.
5. _____ you asked your parents for permission to go?
6. By tomorrow, she certainly _____ _____ had her audition.
7. We _____ not going to the state fair this year.
8. My mother _____ _____ finished baking by now.
9. This poor paper _____ _____ written over.
10. I _____ _____ carefully prepared for this exam.

3.1 Adjectives as Modifiers

Adjectives with Nouns and Pronouns

An adjective is used to describe a noun or pronoun. Adjectives answer the questions *What kind? Which one? How many?* or *How much?* about the nouns or pronouns they modify.

ADJECTIVE QUESTIONS		
What kind?	*white* fence	*unhappy* child
Which one?	*this* photo	*each* one
How many?	*two* snacks	*many* others
How much?	*enough* time	*more* examples

EXERCISE A: Recognizing Adjectives and the Words They Modify. In the sentences below underline each adjective and circle the noun or pronoun it modifies.

EXAMPLE: A hungry lion stalked the frightened animals.

1. Laura bought a blue blouse with white lace trimmings.
2. Several athletes complained about the old stadium.
3. The writer, tall and impressive, entered the auditorium.
4. Each one in the class will develop an original project.
5. I made three attempts to reach the local representative.
6. A gracious hostess greeted us at the flower show.
7. The branches, dry and peeling, showed the effects of the drought.
8. We packed the fragile glassware in a reinforced container.
9. The investigator hopes to get some answers from the lone witness.
10. The decorator suggested using three large paintings to cover the bare wall.

EXERCISE B: Using Adjectives in Sentences. Complete the sentences below by filling in an appropriate adjective in each blank space.

EXAMPLE: My _____ car is equipped with _____ tires.
My _*foreign*_ car is equipped with _*radial*_ tires.

1. An _____ teacher scolded the _____ student.
2. My mother just bought a _____ _____ suit.
3. Maxwell Elementary School, _____ and _____, will soon be closed.
4. A _____ visitors waited to see the _____ prime minister.
5. The front of the house is painted _____ and _____ .
6. This _____ edition of the book is _____ .
7. Do you have _____ time to reach the _____ speaker?
8. _____ police cars followed the _____ van.
9. _____ one is by far the _____ version.
10. A _____ , _____ crowd greeted the hero.

3.1 Adjectives as Modifiers

Articles

The definite article, *the,* refers to a specific person, place, or thing. The indefinite articles, *a* and *an,* refer to any one of a class of people, places, or things. *A* is used before consonant sounds. *An* is used before vowel sounds.

USING *A* AND *AN*	
Consonant Sounds	**Vowel Sounds**
a *cold* drink	an *envelope*
a *hammer* (*h* sound)	an *honorary* guest (no *h* sound)
a *one-sided* game	an *oboe* (*o* sound)
(*w* sound)	an *unlikely* event (*u* sound)
a *unicorn* (*y* sound)	

Nouns Used as Adjectives

Nouns are sometimes used as adjectives. When a noun is used as an adjective, it comes before another noun and answers the question *What kind?* or *Which one?*

Nouns	Used as Adjectives
river	river bank (*What kind* of bank?)
bottle	bottle opener (*Which* opener?)

EXERCISE A: Using the Indefinite Articles *A* and *An* Correctly. In the space provided, place the article *a* or *an.*

EXAMPLE: __an__ old person   __a__ happy audience

1. ____ honest woman
2. ____ compound verb
3. ____ union meeting
4. ____ only child
5. ____ uneasy parent
6. ____ one-time experience
7. ____ horse trade
8. ____ egg salad sandwich
9. ____ helping hand
10. ____ uniform test

EXERCISE B: Recognizing Nouns Used As Adjectives. In each sentence below underline the noun used as an adjective and circle the noun it modifies.

EXAMPLE: This is the only __food__ (market) for a while.

1. How often do you play table tennis?
2. Our village square is two blocks from here.
3. My older sister joined an exclusive supper club.
4. Speak to the organizers about making a rule change.
5. The producer was not pleased with the audience participation.
6. A new work order arrived this morning.
7. For my birthday my brother bought me a new desk lamp.
8. With a black and red typewriter ribbon you can achieve special effects.
9. The basketball game was suddenly canceled.
10. Which radio station do you listen to the most?

3.1 Adjectives as Modifiers

Proper Adjectives

A proper adjective is a proper noun used as an adjective or an adjective formed from a proper noun.

Proper Nouns as Proper Adjectives	Proper Adjectives from Proper Nouns
Kennedy memoirs	Congressional elections
Brooklyn Bridge celebration	Shakespearean costumes
Chicago meeting	Indian customs

Compound Adjectives

A compound adjective is an adjective made up of more than one word.

Hyphenated Compound Adjectives	Combined Compound Adjectives
three-piece suit	newspaper reporter
full-time job	schoolwide project

EXERCISE A: Recognizing Proper Adjectives. Underline the proper adjective in each sentence below and circle the noun it modifies.

EXAMPLE: A <u>Kansas</u> (tornado) destroyed three towns.

 1. The Senate committee adjourned the hearing.
 2. My uncle just recorded a Beethoven symphony.
 3. Our Canadian relatives will arrive next week.
 4. Did you see the last Super Bowl special?
 5. My social studies report is on Victorian traditions.
 6. This new restaurant features American favorites.
 7. A Chicago group wants to purchase land in our area.
 8. I found that *Newsday* article fascinating.
 9. The Russian ballet will appear in Los Angeles soon.
10. The general manager canceled the Monday meeting.

EXERCISE B: Recognizing Compound Adjectives. Underline the compound adjective in each sentence below and circle the noun it modifies.

EXAMPLE: <u>Hyperactive</u> (children) often need treatment.

 1. Have you ever taken a multiple-choice test?
 2. We invited a professional football player to visit us.
 3. Our next guest will be a well-known actress.
 4. When do we change to daylight-saving time?
 5. My talented aunt is designing a crisscross pattern.
 6. We have just formed a cleanup squad.
 7. Our inept team actually scored a first-quarter touchdown.
 8. I have two nearsighted brothers.
 9. We have planned a life-size statue of Winston Churchill.
10. People are afraid he will be a rubber-stamp legislator.

3.2 | Pronouns Used as Adjectives

Possessive Adjectives

A pronoun is used as an adjective if it modifies a noun. A personal pronoun used as a possessive adjective answers the question *Which one?* about a noun that follows it.

POSSESSIVE ADJECTIVES			
my	his	its	their
your	her	our	

Demonstrative Adjectives

The four demonstrative pronouns—*this, that, these,* and *those*—can also be used as demonstrative adjectives.

DEMONSTRATIVE ADJECTIVES
I want *this* one.
She chose *that* car.
These apples are sour.
Did you read *those* notes?

EXERCISE A: Recognizing Possessive and Demonstrative Adjectives. Underline the possessive or demonstrative adjective in each sentence below and circle the noun it modifies.

EXAMPLE: The committee chose those colors.

1. Have you explained their responsibilities to them?
2. Everyone found his report terribly upsetting.
3. Unfortunately, those cartons are blocking the main entrance.
4. This short story by Pearl Buck has a surprise ending.
5. Did you speak to your grandmother last night?
6. Maureen has wanted that jacket for a long time.
7. If you are interested, I will show you my camera.
8. All of these recipes are sugar-free.
9. I really wanted to give them our opinion first.
10. I think her graphic will certainly win a prize.

EXERCISE B: Using Possessive and Demonstrative Adjectives in Sentences. Fill in the blank in each sentence below with appropriate possessive or demonstrative adjectives.

EXAMPLE: We explained ___our___ idea to them.

1. _____ manual explains what you have to do.
2. Later, I told them _____ plans for the new theater.
3. Have you found _____ glasses yet?
4. I suggest that you study _____ charts carefully.
5. Paula described _____ frightening experience to us.
6. You can redeem _____ coupons in the supermarket.
7. Before they left, they paid for _____ tickets.
8. My father asked me to send you _____ best wishes.
9. All of _____ cars have diesel engines.
10. _____ explanation seems to be incorrect.

3.2 Pronouns Used as Adjectives

Interrogative Adjectives

Three interrogative pronouns—*which, what,* and *whose*—can be used as interrogative adjectives.

INTERROGATIVE PRONOUNS
Which member of the team scored the most points?
What kind of hiking boots did you buy?
Whose composition was read aloud in class?

Indefinite Adjectives

Some indefinite pronouns can also be used as indefinite adjectives. Some indefinite adjectives can be used only with singular nouns, some only with plural nouns, and some with both.

INDEFINITE ADJECTIVES
Used with Singular Nouns: another, each, either, neither
Used with Plural Nouns: both, few, several, many
Used with Singular or Plural Nouns: all, any, more, most, other, some

EXERCISE A: Recognizing Interrogative and Indefinite Adjectives. Underline the interrogative or indefinite adjective in each sentence below and circle the noun it modifies. Be prepared to tell whether the pronoun is indefinite or interrogative.

EXAMPLE: Each (visitor) was given a souvenir.

1. Both singers gave outstanding performances tonight.
2. Whose report did you like the best?
3. I still expect to read another book this week.
4. There are many explanations for her absence.
5. Chris suggested many ideas which could work.
6. Several doctors attended the patient.
7. Most visitors to the country fair were pleased with the exhibits.
8. Have you developed some new styles recently?
9. All indications point to a glorious victory.
10. What excuse will the principal offer the students?

EXERCISE B: Using Interrogative and Indefinite Adjectives in Sentences. Fill in the blank in each sentence below with an appropriate interrogative or indefinite adjective.

EXAMPLE: I just can't give them ___*other*___ topics.

1. _____ countries would you like to visit this summer?
2. My guess is that there are only a _____ possibilities.
3. _____ contestant will sing two numbers.
4. I know _____ students who will participate.
5. Bill asked _____ sisters to go to the junior high dance.
6. _____ Mark or Todd will represent our class.
7. _____ dictionary did she borrow?
8. _____ explanation is better than none.
9. We waited _____ hours for them to arrive.
10. _____ sport will rival basketball at our school?

4.1 | Adverbs as Modifiers

Adverbs Modifying Verbs

Adverbs modify verbs, adjectives, or other adverbs. An adverb modifying a verb will answer one of four questions about the verb: *Where? When? In what manner?* or *To what extent?*

ADVERBS MODIFYING VERBS	
Where?	**When?**
jogged *here* signaled *left*	arrive *tonight* will speak *soon*
In What Manner?	**To What Extent**
smiled *happily* *willingly* gave	*hardly* know explained *completely*

EXERCISE A: Recognizing Adverbs That Modify Verbs. Underline the adverb in each sentence. In the space provided, indicate which question the adverb answers: *where? when? in what manner?* or *to what extent?*

EXAMPLE: They <u>nearly</u> had an accident. ___*to what extent?*___

1. I arrive early at school on Fridays. _____
2. To reach the mall, turn left at the light. _____
3. Everyone reacted sadly to the news. _____
4. My brother will be going away to college. _____
5. Do you thoroughly understand your task? _____
6. Bring all the reference books here. _____
7. I cautiously opened the door to the barn. _____
8. Nina is barely acquainted with them. _____
9. I will drive tomorrow to the festival. _____
10. The train suddenly jolted to a halt. _____

EXERCISE B: Writing Original Sentences with Adverbs. Use each adverb below in an original sentence. Make certain that the adverb modifies the verb.

EXAMPLE: nearly ___*My grandmother nearly slipped on the ice.*___

1. quickly _____.
2. here _____.
3. completely _____.
4. soon _____.
5. away _____.
6. easily _____.
7. tomorrow _____.
8. almost _____.
9. quietly _____.
10. hardly _____.

4.1 Adverbs as Modifiers

Adverbs Modifying Adjectives

An adverb modifying an adjective answers the question *To what extent?*

ADVERBS MODIFYING ADJECTIVES	
often ready	*extremely* helpful
too late	*scarcely* prepared

Adverbs Modifying Other Adverbs

An adverb modifying another adverb also answers the question *To what extent?*

ADVERBS MODIFYING ADVERBS	
moves *quite* rapidly	visits *less* regularly
drives *more* carefully	speaks *very* slowly

EXERCISE A: Recognizing the Words Adverbs Modify. On the blank at the right, write whether each underlined adverb modifies an adjective or another adverb.

EXAMPLE: Her coat appears <u>rather</u> short.   _adjective_

1. Bob should learn to speak <u>more</u> clearly. _____

2. The senator was <u>nearly</u> late for his meeting. _____

3. The patient's reactions seem <u>rather</u> slow. _____

4. Her explanation is <u>perfectly</u> correct. _____

5. The doctor arrived <u>very</u> quickly at the accident. _____

6. Yes, I am <u>somewhat</u> embarrassed at his actions. _____

7. My best friend is <u>often</u> absent from school. _____

8. For my taste she plays <u>too</u> rapidly. _____

9. We receive a new shipment <u>almost</u> weekly. _____

10. At her audition Carrie seemed <u>slightly</u> upset. _____

EXERCISE B: Adding Adverbs to Sentences. Fill in the blank in each sentence with an adverb that answers the question *To what extent?* Circle the word it modifies.

EXAMPLE: This road is ___often___ (deserted) at night.

1. Richard seemed _____ disturbed at the news.

2. _____ early in her speech, she began to stumble.

3. My older sister swims _____ rapidly.

4. The federal agents approached the building _____ cautiously.

5. John played his clarinet _____ well.

6. After the trip my grandmother looked _____ tired.

7. Response time to fires is now _____ more rapid.

8. Finally, the family is _____ ready to go.

9. Tom plays shortstop _____ awkwardly.

10. This salesman is _____ late for appointments.

4.2 Adverbs Used in Sentences

Finding Adverbs in Sentences

Adverbs can be located in almost any part of a sentence: at the beginning or end of a sentence; before, after, or between the parts of a verb; before an adjective; and before another adverb.

FINDING ADVERBS	
Suddenly, they appeared. I am *not* surprised.	My cousin smiled *happily.* She is *rather* tall.

Adverb or Adjective?

Some words can be either adverbs or adjectives. Remember that an adverb modifies a verb, an adjective, or another adverb. An adjective modifies a noun or a pronoun.

Adverbs	Adjectives
Our team plays *hard.* She exercises *daily.*	We also use a *hard* ball. We have a *daily* drill.

EXERCISE A: Finding Adverbs in Sentences. Locate the adverbs in these sentences. Underline the adverbs and circle the words they modify.

EXAMPLE: At the debate you (must speak) clearly.

1. Surprisingly, I finished my homework in a hour.
2. I have often wondered about her past.
3. We have changed our minds completely.
4. Our new math teacher is extremely pleasant.
5. The gymnast performed all her tasks smoothly.
6. Unfortunately, the bad weather prevented the picnic.
7. On Saturdays, Bill and Phil thoroughly clean their apartment.
8. Gloria has not forgotten the insult.
9. My dance teacher always agrees to perform for us.
10. After a little work, the engine purred smoothly.

EXERCISE B: Distinguishing Between Adjectives and Adverbs. In the space provided, write whether the underlined word is an adjective or an adverb.

EXAMPLE: We have a <u>weekly</u> conference.   *adjective*

1. On the day of the fair Sandy awoke <u>early</u>. _____
2. My sister has always been a <u>fast</u> eater. _____
3. I have an uncle who sings <u>beautifully</u>. _____
4. We bought Mom a <u>lovely</u> present for her birthday. _____
5. Our insurance salesmen work <u>late</u> twice a week. _____
6. Make certain to give the squad leader an <u>early</u> signal. _____
7. Our Spanish teacher speaks too <u>fast</u>. _____
8. For breakfast I usually eat a <u>hard</u> roll. _____
9. My friend lives <u>close</u> to the racetrack. _____
10. Sam had an extremely <u>close</u> call this morning. _____

5.1 Prepositions

Words Used as Prepositions

Prepositions are words such as *in, at, from, ahead of,* and *next to.* A preposition relates the noun or pronoun following it to another word in the sentence.

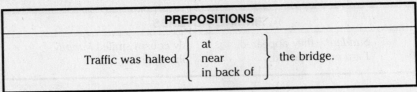

PREPOSITIONS		
Traffic was halted	at near in back of	the bridge.

Prepositional Phrases

A prepositional phrase is a group of words that includes a preposition and a noun or pronoun called the object of the preposition.

PREPOSITIONAL PHRASES	
Prepositions	**Objects of the Prepositions**
across	the *street*
between	*us*
next to	the old *statue*

EXERCISE A: Identifying Prepositions. Underline each preposition in the sentences below. Some sentences have more than one.

EXAMPLE: <u>Without</u> oxygen she will never make it <u>to</u> the hospital.

1. I placed the lawn mower in a corner of the garage.
2. During the spring I often visit a flower show.
3. A man from the IRS called father at home.
4. She finally agreed in spite of her original protests.
5. Father is not terribly worried about them.
6. You will find extremely poor construction behind the wall.
7. Is this complicated project beyond them?
8. The invading army marched into the valley without warning.
9. The book is underneath the pillow near the headboard.
10. In addition to having bad manners, she leaves her clothes on the floor.

EXERCISE B: Identifying Prepositional Phrases. Place parentheses around each prepositional phrase. Underline each preposition and circle its object. Some sentences have more than one prepositional phrase.

EXAMPLE: (<u>In</u> the ⃝morning⃝) we left (<u>for</u> ⃝San Diego⃝).

1. From the meeting we strolled into the restaurant.
2. We listened intently throughout the manager's presentation.
3. A group of students demonstrated in front of the building.
4. As of this morning, the game was canceled.
5. At dawn we attempted to swim across the river.
6. The investigators from the police found evidence under the bridge.
7. We raced through the enemy town at great speed.
8. Instead of hamburgers, we had salads for lunch.
9. The road marker is some distance in front of the chalet.
10. According to the travel agent, we should arrive about noon.

5.1 | Prepositions

Preposition or Adverb?

Some words can be either prepositions or adverbs, depending on how they are used. A preposition will always be followed by a noun or pronoun used as an object. Adverbs modify verbs and have no objects.

Prepositions	Adverbs
She peered *across* the *lake*.	Mary will look *across*.
The note is *inside* the *box*.	Please wait *inside*.
The car streaked *past us*.	The prisoner slipped *past*.

EXERCISE A: Distinguishing Between Prepositions and Adverbs. Write whether the underlined word in each sentence is a preposition or an adverb.

EXAMPLE: My cousin wriggled and tried to slide <u>through</u>. _____*adverb*_____

1. I casually strolled <u>through</u> the entrance. _____
2. <u>Around</u> our house we always have excitement. _____
3. We were told to travel <u>along</u> this road for two miles. _____
4. From the bridge Susan tried to look <u>underneath</u>. _____
5. Do you think you can walk <u>past</u> the guards? _____
6. <u>Behind</u> the closet is a secret passageway. _____
7. After ten hours of work Tom was finally <u>through</u>. _____
8. Walk <u>around</u> and see if you can spot mother. _____
9. An angry crowd surged <u>near</u> the governor. _____
10. Pass <u>along</u> until you reach the sentry at the gate. _____

EXERCISE B: Adding Prepositions and Adverbs to Sentences. The sentences below are grouped in pairs. For each pair, select a word that fits appropriately and write it in the spaces provided. Label the adverb *A* and the preposition *P*.

EXAMPLE: Walk <u>over</u>. ____*A*____
Throw the ball <u>over</u> the fence. ____*P*____

1. a. Your best friend is _____ the phone. _____
   b. Keep your sweater _____. _____
2. a. Please come _____. _____
   b. We have a canopy _____ the window. _____
3. a. Keep searching. You will find the recipe _____. _____
   b. The emergency hose is _____ the radiator. _____
4. a. I hope to see them _____. _____
   b. The curio shop happens to be _____ the corner. _____
5. a. Don't forget to turn the lights _____. _____
   b. Paint has begun to chip _____ the wall. _____

5.2 Conjunctions

Coordinating Conjunctions

Coordinating conjunctions connect similar words. They will connect two or more nouns, adjectives, or verbs. They can also connect larger groups of words, such as phrases, or even sentences.

COORDINATING CONJUNCTIONS			
and	for	or	yet
but	nor	so	

Correlative Conjunctions

Correlative conjunctions come in pairs. They connect the same kinds of similar words or groups of words as do coordinating conjunctions.

CORRELATIVE CONJUNCTIONS		
both . . . and either . . . or	not only . . . but also	neither . . . nor whether . . . or

EXERCISE A: Identifying Coordinating and Correlative Conjunctions. Find and circle the conjunctions below. Write *C* for each coordinating conjunction and *COR* for correlative conjunctions.

EXAMPLE: (Both) Sylvia (and) I will participate. _____COR_____

1. Neither my brother nor my sister is eager to go. _____
2. I would like to buy a new stereo, but I can't afford to. _____
3. For our surprise party the entire family cooked and baked. _____
4. Either Stan or Bobby will run the final lap in the race. _____
5. Not only was I surprised, but I was also disappointed. _____
6. Marie kept working, for she knew her deadline was close. _____
7. We intend to visit both Toronto and Ottawa. _____
8. Whether Diane or Annette represents us is unimportant. _____
9. My brother will sing or play the saxophone. _____
10. Our old car is large yet economical. _____

EXERCISE B: Writing Original Sentences Using Conjunctions. Use each conjunction below in an original sentence. Remember that you can connect nouns, verbs, adjectives, phrases, or sentences.

EXAMPLE: nor _*I won't drive, nor will I take a train*_ .

1. but _____
2. both . . . and _____
3. or _____
4. either . . . or _____
5. yet _____
6. whether . . . or _____
7. and _____
8. neither . . . nor _____
9. for _____
10. not only . . . but also _____

5.2 | Conjunctions

Subordinating Conjunctions

Subordinating conjunctions connect two ideas by making one idea less important than the other.

FREQUENTLY USED SUBORDINATING CONJUNCTIONS			
after	as though	since	until
although	because	so that	when
as	before	than	whenever
as if	even though	though	wherever
as soon as	if	unless	while

EXERCISE A: Recognizing Subordinating Conjunctions. Circle the subordinating conjunction in each sentence below. Then underline the dependent idea that follows it.

EXAMPLE: (When) I received the package, I jumped for joy.

1. Mother entered the store while everyone else waited in the car.
2. Although I understand his reason, I cannot accept his poor behavior.
3. Unless I hear from the committee tomorrow, I will change my plans.
4. Uncle Bob always phones whenever he is in town.
5. I can't go to the concert because I have to study for my finals.
6. Even though I enjoy some of the new musical groups, I don't think any group can replace the Beatles.
7. Unless we notify the book club, we will continue to get a new book each month.
8. Melody will bring us the tomato plants as soon as she returns from Boston.
9. Mother wants a new car so that she can drive herself to work.
10. Our team can win the championship if it continues to train hard.

EXERCISE B: Writing Sentences Using Conjunctions. Fill in the blanks with words that will complete each sentence. All three kinds of conjunctions are included below.

EXAMPLE: ___I will polish the car___ since ___Father needs it tomorrow___.

1. When _____, _____.
2. _____ so that _____.
3. Either _____ or _____.
4. _____, but _____.
5. Unless _____, _____.
6. Both _____ and _____.
7. _____ even though _____.
8. If _____, _____.
9. _____, or _____.
10. Whenever _____, _____
_____.

5.3 Interjections

Using Interjections

An interjection expresses feeling or emotion and functions independently of a sentence. It is set off from the rest of the sentence with an exclamation mark or a comma.

EXPRESSING EMOTION WITH INTERJECTIONS	
Emotion	**Interjection**
Surprise	*Gee,* I never expected to see you today.
Joy	*Hurray!* We won.
Pain	*Ouch,* I hurt my finger.
Impatience	*Darn,* I missed my train.
Hesitation	We, *uh,* think you're wrong.

EXERCISE A: Recognizing Interjections. Underline the interjection in each sentence. In the space provided, write which emotion the interjection conveys.

EXAMPLE: <u>Wow!</u> I never expected a fur coat.   _____surprise_____

1. Hey! Keep your hands off that camera. _____

2. "Goodness," exclaimed Grandmother. "I never expected to see you all

    today." _____

3. Darn, Alice is late again. _____

4. Gee, I won a prize in the lottery. _____

5. Uh, I'm afraid I've forgotten your name. _____

EXERCISE B: Using Interjections in Sentences. Use the following interjections with commas or exclamation marks in sentences of your own.

EXAMPLE: hey
    Hey, watch where you are parking!

1. whew _____

2. oh _____

3. ouch _____

4. ugh _____

5. hurray _____

6. wow _____

7. goodness _____

8. darn _____

9. well _____

10. golly _____

6.1 Determining Parts of Speech

Identifying Parts of Speech in Sentences

The way a word is used in a sentence determines its part of speech.

WORDS USED DIFFERENTLY
As a Noun: I often relax with a good *book*. *As a Verb:* As a travel agent, I *book* trips daily. *As an Adjective:* All she really has is *book* knowledge.

EXERCISE A: Identifying Parts of Speech. In the space provided, write the part of speech of the underlined word in each sentence.

EXAMPLE: They now <u>head</u> an important company.   *verb*
             In the accident she injured her <u>head</u>.   *noun*

1. From the ledge can you see <u>below</u>? _____
2. <u>Below</u> the main level, we have a large playroom. _____
3. Can you see the <u>outside</u> wall clearly? _____
4. The <u>outside</u> of the building is all brick. _____
5. The assistant principal said, "Please wait <u>outside</u>." _____
6. I offered them <u>several</u> maps of the state. _____
7. <u>Several</u> of the students visited the museum. _____
8. In this job we <u>train</u> salesmen for six weeks. _____
9. I think Aunt Betty called from the <u>train</u> station. _____
10. Which <u>train</u> is an express to the city? _____
11. We <u>second</u> Jerry's nomination for president. _____
12. The dean is willing to give you a <u>second</u> chance. _____
13. I will be finished in a <u>second</u>. _____
14. What is the <u>call</u> number of that book? _____
15. Later, we will <u>call</u> them with the good news. _____
16. Thinking it over, she finally walked <u>across</u>. _____
17. The doctor's office is <u>across</u> the hall. _____
18. We sent the starving people <u>care</u> packages. _____
19. Our students <u>care</u> deeply about their friends. _____
20. Today, we will discuss the <u>care</u> of eyes and ears. _____

EXERCISE B: Using Words as Different Parts of Speech. In the space provided write sentences that use the words below as the parts of speech given in parentheses.

EXAMPLE: test (noun)   *She failed another test.*
             test (verb)   *We test each unit several times.*

1. around (preposition) _____
2. around (adverb) _____
3. name (adjective) _____
4. name (noun) _____
5. name (verb) _____

7.1 The Basic Sentence

The Two Basic Elements of a Sentence

All sentences must contain two basic elements—a subject and a verb. The subject answers the question *Who?* or *What?* before the verb. The verb tells what the subject does, what is done to the subject, or the subject's condition.

SUBJECTS AND VERBS
Dogs of all kinds were enrolled in the obedience class.
Carefully, he removed the painting from the crate.
Lara has not been practicing the piano regularly.

The Need to Express a Complete Thought

A sentence must express a complete thought. A group of words with a subject and verb expresses a complete thought if it can stand by itself and still make sense.

COMPLETE THOUGHTS
Incomplete Thought: The senator from New Jersey
Complete Thought: The senator from New Jersey raced to the airport to catch a plane.

EXERCISE A: Recognizing Subjects and Verbs. Underline each subject once and each verb twice in the sentences below.

EXAMPLE: In the morning we began our trip.

1. An angry principal addressed the student body.
2. Hannibal was one of the greatest generals of all time.
3. A halfback with great speed is the dream of every coach.
4. In a glass tube, neon emits an orange glow.
5. My bad ankle is bothering me once again.
6. A bottle of shampoo just broke.
7. A rolltop oak desk is one of our family's heirlooms.
8. My sister just bought three new record albums.
9. Nehru became prime minister of India in 1947.
10. The road to the battleground is winding and dangerous.

EXERCISE B: Recognizing Complete Sentences. Only five of the following groups of words are sentences. If the sentence is complete, write a *C*. If the group of words is not a complete sentence, write *NC*.

EXAMPLE: If the fire department does not come at once.   *NC*

1. Leslie borrowed two reference books from the library. _____
2. Whenever I go to the movies with my friends. _____
3. We decided to prune all the rose bushes. _____
4. Vincenzo Bellini is a famous Italian operatic composer. _____
5. At the end of the road near the Graham Bridge. _____
6. Because she wanted to do well on the test. _____
7. Bobby and Marie decided to shovel the snow. _____
8. A long report about problems in the environment. _____
9. Since I am very much interested in biology. _____
10. We cannot depend any longer on our old car. _____

7.2 Complete Subjects and Predicates

Finding Complete Subjects and Predicates

Every sentence can be divided into two parts—a complete subject and a complete predicate. The complete subject consists of the subject and any words related to it. The complete predicate consists of the verb and any words related to it.

Complete Subject	Complete Predicate
Most <u>clerks</u>	<u>answer</u> questions.
Most <u>clerks</u> in the City Hall	<u>answer</u> questions cheerfully about taxes and unpaid bills.

EXERCISE A: Recognizing Complete Subjects and Complete Predicates. Underline the subject once and the verb twice. Then draw a vertical line between the complete subject and the complete predicate.

EXAMPLE: The <u>mayor</u> of the city | <u>addressed</u> the civics club.

1. Our gnarled apple tree was destroyed in the storm.
2. Ribbons of water cascaded down the mountainside.
3. Our new teacher explained her requirements for a notebook.
4. The Chicago Cubs for many years played only in daylight.
5. A colorful Thanksgiving Day parade always brings out a crowd.
6. Our new uniforms were lost somehow during the summer.
7. The computer in mother's office has an expensive printer.
8. The background of the flag of Nova Scotia is white.
9. Some news photos remain in your mind for years.
10. A brilliant sunset filled the sky with a splash of reds, yellows, and oranges.

EXERCISE B: Adding Complete Subjects or Complete Predicates. Each item below contains either a complete subject or a complete predicate. Supply the missing part.

EXAMPLE: ___My old friend Dave___ entered the supermarket.

1. The throne in the center of the stage_____.
2. _____ welcomed the incoming class.
3. Our football coach_____.
4. _____ was extremely difficult to explain.
5. My favorite experiment in science_____.
6. _____ is much greater than before.
7. Our local post office_____.
8. _____ is a book I will never forget.
9. Next year in the spring I_____.
10. _____ should win a championship.

7.3 Compound Subjects and Verbs

Compound Subjects

A compound subject is two or more subjects that have the same verb and are joined by a conjunction such as *and* or *or*.

COMPOUND SUBJECTS
<u>History</u> and <u>science</u> <u>are</u> my favorites.
<u>Judy, David,</u> and <u>Charles</u> <u>will travel</u> to Philadelphia.

Compound Verbs

A compound verb is two or more verbs that have the same subject and are joined by a conjunction such as *and* or *or*.

COMPOUND VERBS
<u>Uncle Steve</u> <u>will fly</u> or <u>drive</u> to the wedding.
My <u>grandmother</u> still <u>bakes</u>, <u>cooks</u>, and <u>sews</u> as much as ever.

EXERCISE A: Recognizing Compound Subjects. In each sentence below underline the compound subject.

EXAMPLE: A <u>bus</u> or <u>train</u> will get you to Memphis.

1. Jo Ann and I often do our research together.
2. A desk blotter and some correction fluid can be purchased here.
3. In the accident Bob and Billy were slightly injured.
4. Ice cream, cookies, or pie will make excellent desserts.
5. In our English class, spelling and grammar are not popular.
6. Snakes, spiders, and assorted rodents infest this forest.
7. His neck and my neck are about the same size.
8. Boston, Philadelphia, and New York are all historic cities.
9. My parents, my grandparents, and my Aunt Sue will spend the summer together.
10. A high fever and a strange rash were the principal symptoms.

EXERCISE B: Recognizing Compound Verbs. In each sentence below underline the compound verb twice.

EXAMPLE: The book <u>opens</u> and <u>closes</u> with a battle scene.

1. My brother sketches or paints almost every day.
2. The child opened the package and reached inside.
3. We walked to the beach, sat for a while in the sun, and took several cold dips.
4. The eagle soared in the sky and then suddenly dove after a prey.
5. The tin roof shook and rattled all night during the storm.
6. My friends bought several albums and had lunch in a hamburger place.
7. The main highway continues this way and then narrows into two lanes.
8. The President will arrive at nine and enter the convention hall a short time later.
9. After school, I do my homework, finish my chores, and watch TV.
10. Mom searched for her slippers and found them under the couch.

7.4 Special Problems with Subjects

Subjects in Orders and Directions

In sentences that give orders or directions, the subject is understood to be *you*.

ORDERS AND DIRECTIONS
(You) <u>Chew</u> your food slowly.
Frank, (you) <u>sit</u> down!
After jogging, (you) <u>take</u> a shower.

Subjects in Questions

In questions the subject often follows the verb or part of the verb.

QUESTIONS
<u>Is</u> the <u>package</u> ready?
<u>Have</u> <u>you</u> <u>found</u> your ring?
When <u>will</u> the <u>senator</u> <u>speak</u>?

EXERCISE A: Recognizing Subjects That Give Orders or Directions. Underline the verb in each sentence with a double line. Write the subject in the space provided. (Four of the sentences do not give orders or directions.)

EXAMPLE: <u>Open</u> the package quickly. ___*you*___

1. Turn right at the traffic light near the mall. _____
2. Jennie, try to concentrate now. _____
3. In the morning Alice often sunbathes. _____
4. After changing the baby, warm up her milk. _____
5. Please wait for the light to change. _____
6. Remember to get a fresh bread and a bag of potatoes. _____
7. The radio slipped off the counter and broke. _____
8. Every morning brush your teeth carefully. _____
9. Dr. Slovak, phone your office now. _____
10. The name of the hotel was recently changed. _____

EXERCISE B: Finding the Subject in Questions. Underline the subjects in the questions below.

EXAMPLE: Whom did the <u>reporter</u> meet?

1. Has the principal entered the auditorium yet?
2. Who is the governor of Arizona?
3. What do you expect to happen tomorrow?
4. Can the vegetables survive a three week drought?
5. Have Dick and Lucy visited the exhibit?
6. Why have they attempted to stop our demonstration?
7. When did the second message reach you?
8. Which chapter of the book is the best?
9. Did both teams arrive simultaneously?
10. Is this the way to spell her name?

7.4 Special Problems with Subjects

Subjects in Sentences Beginning with *There* or *Here*

There or *here* is never the subject of a sentence. Sentences beginning with *there* or *here* are in inverted word order. The subject will come after the verb.

SENTENCES BEGINNING WITH *THERE* OR *HERE*
There <u>are</u> two <u>telegrams</u> in your office.
Here <u>is</u> the <u>message</u>.

Subjects in Sentences Inverted for Emphasis

There are also other sentences with inverted word order. In these sentences the subject follows the verb in order to receive greater emphasis.

OTHER SENTENCES IN INVERTED WORD ORDER
In her eyes <u>was</u> <u>fear</u>.
At the fork <u>is</u> a <u>police station</u>.

EXERCISE A: Recognizing Subjects in Sentences with Inverted Word Order. Underline the subject once and the verb twice in each sentence below.

EXAMPLE: Near the beach <u>is</u> an old <u>bathhouse</u>.

1. There is a lesson to be learned from this.
2. At the top of the hill stands an impressive statue.
3. Here are the keys to the car.
4. From the burning building came a shout of a child.
5. There is too much confusion about your plan.
6. With her was a girl from college.
7. Out of the backfield raced Bob with the ball.
8. Here was a striking bit of evidence.
9. In the center of the ceiling was a listening device.
10. There should be a box of tools in the cellar.

EXERCISE B: Writing Original Sentences in Inverted Word Order. Write sentences that begin with the words below. Make certain that the verb comes before the subject.

EXAMPLE: There _____
            There _*is your lost ring.*_

1. Here _____.
2. Near the top of the hill _____.
3. With them _____.
4. There _____.
5. In this story _____.
6. Over there _____.
7. Under my bed _____.
8. Near the railroad station _____.
9. In the truck _____.
10. In her wallet _____.

7.5 Direct Objects

The Direct Object

A direct object is a noun or pronoun that receives the action of a transitive verb.

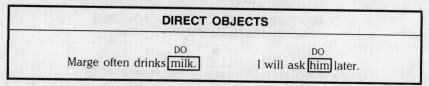

Compound Direct Objects

A compound direct object is two or more nouns or pronouns that receive the action of the same transitive verb.

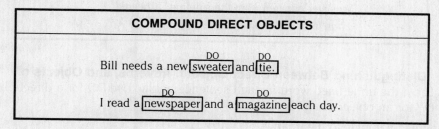

EXERCISE A: Recognizing Direct Objects. Circle the direct object or the compound direct objects in each sentence.

EXAMPLE: Jay told Carol and her about it.

1. We will plan the project for the fair carefully.
2. The next morning Sally took her driving test.
3. Gloria expects them to arrive at seven.
4. She bought gloves, a scarf, and two skirts.
5. I want my parents and my grandparents to know first.
6. Will you write her about your victory?
7. The new car has an automatic transmission and cruise control.
8. My mother injured her hand this morning.
9. For graduation my sister got a new typewriter and a camera.
10. Tell Bill and them to wait for the decision.

EXERCISE B: Using Direct Objects. Fill in the blanks in the sentences below with appropriate direct objects. Use both nouns and pronouns.

EXAMPLE: I reached ___New Haven___ the next day.

1. After two hours I closed the _____.
2. Ask _____ about the second-half comeback.
3. I want _____ and _____ to represent us.
4. Will you remind _____ about the junior high dance?
5. In the bakery, buy some _____, _____, and _____.
6. I saw _____ at the movies yesterday.
7. On the weekend she wrote _____.
8. Do you have _____ for the football game?
9. We will welcome Ben and _____ to our class.
10. Next week Father will build a _____ and a _____.

7.5 Direct Objects

Direct Object, Adverb, or Object of a Preposition

A direct object is never an adverb or the noun or pronoun at the end of a prepositional phrase.

```
COMPARING DIRECT OBJECTS, ADVERBS,
AND OBJECTS OF PREPOSITIONS

                        DO
My sister cheered the team. (Cheered what? team)

                  ADV
My sister cheered wildly. (Cheered what? no direct
object)

                 PREP      OBJ OF PREP
My sister cheered from the sideline. (Cheered
what? no direct object)
```

EXERCISE A: Distinguishing Between Direct Objects, Adverbs, and Objects of Prepositions. Label the underlined word in each sentence below. Use *DO* for a direct object, *ADV* for an adverb, and *OP* for an object of a preposition.

EXAMPLE: We agreed <u>willingly</u> to the change.   _ADV_

1. I really need a new <u>thesaurus</u>. _____
2. At sunset we finally stopped at an old <u>motel</u>. _____
3. For years now my brother has played <u>chess</u>. _____
4. Leaving the plane, the astronaut smiled <u>happily</u>. _____
5. My parents changed their <u>decision</u> without warning. _____
6. The defendant walked <u>wearily</u> into the courtroom. _____
7. I built these oak <u>cabinets</u> without any help. _____
8. Much to my surprise, the book ended <u>strangely</u>. _____
9. Are you still interested in the <u>unknown</u>? _____
10. Last spring she planted <u>tomatoes</u> in her yard. _____

EXERCISE B: Using Direct Objects, Adverbs, and Objects of Prepositions in Sentences. Fill in each blank with the kind of word indicated in the parentheses.

EXAMPLE: (direct object) I often enjoy   _hockey games_   .

1. (adverb) When Uncle Ted arrived, we smiled _____.
2. (direct object) You can buy _____ in any drugstore.
3. (obj. of prep.) The photo you want is in the _____.
4. (direct object) If you go to the post office, I need some _____.
5. (adverb) Speak _____ during your interview.
6. (direct object) Who wrote _____?
7. (obj. of prep.) Wait for us under the _____.
8. (adverb) Bess reacted _____ to the suggestion.
9. (direct object) I put the _____ in the file cabinet.
10. (obj. of prep.) We enjoyed the performer on the _____.

7.5 Direct Objects

Direct Objects in Questions

A direct object in a sentence in normal word order is found after the verb. In a question the direct object is sometimes near the beginning of the sentence, before the verb.

Questions	Normal Word Order
DO **What** will she do now?	DO She will do **what** now.
DO **Whom** do they want?	DO They do want **whom.**
DO Which **road** should we take?	DO We should take which **road.**

EXERCISE A: Finding Direct Objects in Questions. Circle the direct object in each question below. Note that in three of the sentences, the direct object follows the verb.

EXAMPLE: Which (tool) do you need?

1. Whom did they call in Portland?
2. Which photograph did they lose?
3. When will the plumber fix the leaking sink?
4. What excuse can she possibly offer?
5. Which role in *Romeo and Juliet* does he want?
6. When will Sandy send the invitations to her party?
7. Whom does the principal expect?
8. How many record albums do you have?
9. Where will you bake the cookies for our get-together?
10. Which recipe will you use?

EXERCISE B: Using Direct Objects in Sentences. Some of the sentences below are questions; others are not. Fill in an appropriate direct object in each blank space.

EXAMPLE: Which ___train___ will you take to Boston?

1. For the science fair I will build a _____.
2. _____ did they invite to speak?
3. Which _____ by John Steinbeck do you want?
4. When will you prepare the _____?
5. We expect _____ to arrive at the airport tonight.
6. How many _____ do you need?
7. From the top of the hill I can see _____.
8. _____ did the dean scold?
9. Where will you buy the _____?
10. I think I can understand your _____.

7.6 | Indirect Objects

The Indirect Object

An indirect object is a noun or pronoun that comes after an action verb and before a direct object. It names the person or thing that something is given to or done for.

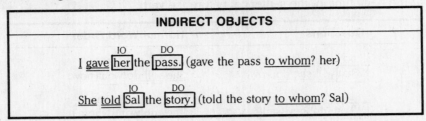

Compound Indirect Objects

A compound indirect object is two or more nouns or pronouns that come after an action verb and before a direct object. It names the persons or things that something is given to or done for.

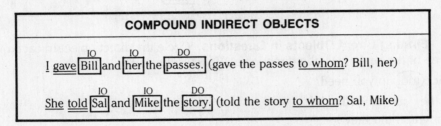

EXERCISE A: Recognizing Indirect Objects. Each sentence below contains a single indirect object or a compound direct object. Circle each indirect object below.

EXAMPLE: I brought (Bill) and (him) tickets.

1. Please take Uncle John his medicine.
2. I will give Jason and Jeffrey their instructions.
3. Did you send Grandfather a post card?
4. Beverly will show the customer the new model.
5. Can you teach us the game?
6. The police told my parents and me the entire story.
7. For Christmas, order Grandpa a new bathrobe.
8. I will sell the developers just a part of the land.
9. In the race you pass Josie the baton.
10. The coach handed Marie and Louise their awards.

EXERCISE B: Recognizing Direct and Indirect Objects. In the sentences below underline the direct objects and circle the indirect objects. Two sentences do not contain an indirect object.

EXAMPLE: Bring (me) the cookbook.

1. From his college my brother sent me a sweatshirt.
2. Pass your aunt the bowl of gravy.
3. We are making our parents a surprise anniversary party.
4. Did you bring your sister a new watch?
5. I will give the detective the information he wants.
6. Mom served our guests her famous rhubarb pie.
7. After much effort, I got the keys to the safe.
8. Have you shown the bus driver the map?
9. The coach offers each candidate two chances to make the team.
10. I asked her for the registration to the car.

7.6 Indirect Objects

Indirect Object or Object of a Preposition?

Do not confuse an indirect object with the object of a preposition. An indirect object never follows the preposition *to* or *for* in a sentence.

```
INDIRECT OBJECT OR PREPOSITIONAL PHRASE?

                  IO              DO
      We brought Mother a beautiful plant.

                              DO      PREP PHRASE
      We brought a beautiful plant to Mother.

              IO          DO
      I prepared them a quick snack.

                        DO    PREP PHRASE
      I prepared a quick snack for them.
```

EXERCISE A: Distinguishing Between Indirect Objects and Objects of Prepositions. In each blank, write whether the underlined word is an indirect object or an object of a preposition.

EXAMPLE: Sally gave the note to <u>Bruce</u>.   *obj. of prep.*

1. I ordered <u>her</u> another pair of sunglasses. _____

2. The principal read <u>us</u> the new regulations. _____

3. Have you given the old lamps to the <u>volunteers</u>? _____

4. I have saved the clippings for <u>her</u>. _____

5. Show your <u>father</u> that strange message. _____

6. In the national park the guide gave a detailed map to <u>him</u>. _____

7. Have you told <u>Donna</u> your startling story? _____

8. She can buy the <u>attendant</u> a present next time. _____

9. The student told an obvious lie to the <u>dean</u>. _____

10. The senior handed the <u>undergraduate</u> the banner. _____

EXERCISE B: Writing Sentences with Indirect Objects and Objects of Prepositions. Rewrite each sentence above. Change each indirect object into a prepositional phrase. Change each prepositional phrase into an indirect object.

EXAMPLE: Sally gave <u>Bruce</u> the note.

1. _____

2. _____

3. _____

4. _____

5. _____

6. _____

7. _____

8. _____

9. _____

10. _____

7.7 | Subject Complements

Predicate Nouns and Pronouns

A subject complement is a noun, pronoun, or adjective that follows a linking verb and tells something about the subject. A predicate noun or predicate pronoun follows a linking verb and renames or identifies the subject of the sentence.

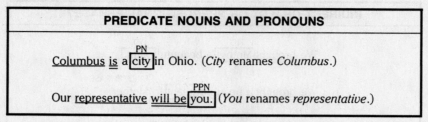

PREDICATE NOUNS AND PRONOUNS

Columbus is a city in Ohio. (*City* renames *Columbus*.)

Our representative will be you. (*You* renames *representative*.)

Predicate Adjectives

A predicate adjective follows a linking verb and describes the subject of the sentence.

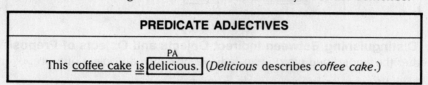

PREDICATE ADJECTIVES

This coffee cake is delicious. (*Delicious* describes *coffee cake*.)

EXERCISE A: Recognizing Predicate Nouns and Predicate Pronouns. In each sentence below underline the predicate noun or predicate pronoun.

EXAMPLE: Melanie should be our <u>captain</u>.

1. Football is my favorite sport in the fall.
2. The brightest student has always been she.
3. New Hampshire has always been a scenic state.
4. Through hard work she became a huge success.
5. John Q. Adams remained a political force all his life.
6. In my new mystery novel, the butler is the murderer.
7. Ronald Reagan became President in 1981.
8. Our old Mercury was a car with an unusually smooth ride.
9. It is she whom our class chose.
10. Mark's idea is an option to consider.

EXERCISE B: Recognizing Predicate Adjectives. In each sentence below underline the predicate adjective.

EXAMPLE: I feel <u>sad</u> about her failure.

1. Churchill's speech was inspiring to the people of London.
2. After the conference they seemed angry at everyone.
3. These curved roads are dangerous after a snow.
4. This old milk tastes sour in my coffee.
5. Barbara is unusually tall for her age.
6. Many of the buildings in this complex are new.
7. The express train seems late tonight.
8. The President appeared nervous in his first debate.
9. Until it was washed, this sweater felt roomy.
10. Your lettering on the poster is very colorful.

7.7 | Subject Complements

Compound Subject Complements

Subject complements can be compound. A compound subject complement consists of two or more predicate nouns, pronouns, or adjectives.

```
COMPOUND SUBJECT COMPLEMENTS

                                    PN         PN
      My two favorite subjects are [math] and [English.]

                                          PPN      PPN
      The speakers at graduation will be [she] and [I.]

                               PA          PA
      His voice tonight seems [deep] and [impressive.]
```

EXERCISE A: Recognizing Compound Subject Complements. Underline the compound subject complement in each sentence. If it consists of predicate nouns, label it *PN*. If it consists of predicate pronouns, label it *PPN*. If it consists of predicate adjectives, label it *PA*.

EXAMPLE: His small room is <u>dark</u> and <u>unpleasant</u>. ___*PA*___

1. The two members of my committee are Les and Sheila. _____
2. I think the winning teams will be they and we. _____
3. The top rated cars were a Toyota, a Buick, and a BMW. _____
4. Until the end, her dance seemed graceful and well executed. _____
5. Unfortunately, it is she and I who resisted. _____
6. This rare stamp must be old and valuable. _____
7. From the box your present is either a camera or a clock radio. _____
8. The strange flower was yellow and orange. _____
9. The finalist must be either he or she. _____
10. Is this telescope Japanese or German? _____

EXERCISE B: Using Compound Subject Complements in Sentences. Fill in the blanks in each sentence with appropriate subject complements. The words in the parentheses will tell you which type to use.

EXAMPLE: (pred. adj.) Her hair is ___*auburn*___ and ___*silky.*___

1. (pred. noun) My favorite actors are _____ and _____.
2. (pred. adj.) In the morning the sea was _____ and _____.
3. (pred. pron.) In the race the winners should be _____ and _____.
4. (pred. noun) She was elected _____ and _____.
5. (pred. adj.) This new camera seems _____ and _____.
6. (pred. pron.) It is _____ and _____ who will go.
7. (pred. noun) The two books I remember best are _____ and _____.
8. (pred. adj.) Are you _____ or _____ now?
9. (pred. pron.) The best artists in the class are _____ and _____.
10. (pred. noun) The two desserts that we will serve at the party are _____ and _____.

7.8 The Four Functions of Sentences

Identifying the Four Functions of Sentences

Sentences are classified according to what they do. There are four types: *declarative, interrogative, imperative,* and *exclamatory.*

THE FOUR FUNCTIONS OF SENTENCES		
Type	**Use**	**Example**
Declarative	States an idea and ends with a period.	Glen Cove has a population of 24,000.
Interrogative	Asks a question and ends with a question mark.	What do you expect to learn?
Imperative	Gives an order or a direction; ends with a period or exclamation mark.	Turn now to the chapter on space exploration. Close the door!
Exclamatory	Conveys a strong emotion and ends with an exclamation mark.	What a total disaster!

EXERCISE A: Recognizing the Four Functions of Sentences. Identify the type of each sentence below. Use a *D* for declarative, an *Int.* for interrogative, an *Imp.* for imperative, and *Exc.* for exclamatory.

EXAMPLE: Who is this strange person? ___*Int.*___

1. Please correct your misspelled words now. _____
2. Ginseng is an herb used for medicinal purposes. _____
3. What a terrible accident! _____
4. Which artist do you admire the most? _____
5. Lillian Gish starred in *The Birth of a Nation.* _____
6. How many records do you have in your collection? _____
7. Drive to the first traffic light and turn right. _____
8. How happy we all are today! _____
9. In Greek mythology Orpheus wrote beautiful music. _____
10. Stop that shouting at once! _____

EXERCISE B: Writing Different Types of Sentences. Write the types of sentences described below.

1. Write a declarative sentence about a famous person.

_____

2. Write a question concerning school work.

_____

3. Write an exclamation about a pleasant event.

_____

4. Write an imperative sentence giving an order or direction.

_____

5. Write a question concerning the future.

_____

7.9 Diagraming Basic Sentence Parts

Subjects and Verbs

In diagraming a sentence, both the subject and the verb are placed on a horizontal line. They are separated by a vertical line, with the subject on the left and the verb on the right.

SUBJECT AND VERB

Flowers bloom.

| Flowers | bloom |

Dean Anderson has been invited.

| Dean Anderson | has been invited |

Adjectives, Adverbs, and Conjunctions

Adjectives are placed on slanted lines directly under the nouns or pronouns they modify. Adverbs are placed on slanted lines directly under the verbs, adjectives, or adverbs they modify. Conjunctions are placed on dotted lines between the words they connect.

ADDING ADJECTIVES AND ADVERBS

An *old, angry* woman complained very *bitterly*.

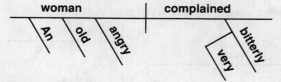

ADDING CONJUNCTIONS

A limping *but* happy runner finished first.

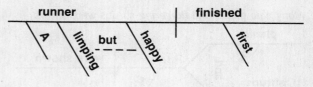

EXERCISE A: Diagraming Subjects and Verbs. Diagram the subjects and verbs below.

1. Lions roar.

2. Jon did agree.

3. She has been chosen.

EXERCISE B: Diagraming Adjectives, Adverbs, and Conjunctions. Diagram each sentence below. Refer to the examples above if necessary.

1. The long, difficult race has finally begun.

2. The tired and hungry child was found later.

3. The show ended very suddenly.

4. The band played noisily but well.

7.9 Diagraming Basic Sentence Parts

Compound Subjects and Verbs

A compound subject has its subject diagramed on two levels. A compound verb is also diagramed on two levels.

COMPOUND SUBJECT

Boys and *girls* were selected.

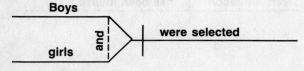

COMPOUND VERB

Students *draw* and *sketch*.

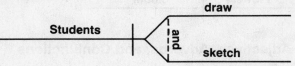

Place any adjective directly under the word it modifies. If an adjective modifies the entire compound subject, place it under the main line. Adverbs are placed directly under the words they modify. If an adverb modifies both verbs, it is placed on the main line.

ADDING ADJECTIVES

Many new plants and *flowering* shrubs were shown.

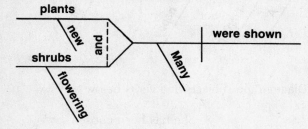

ADDING ADVERBS

Suzy *now* speaks *well* but walks *poorly*.

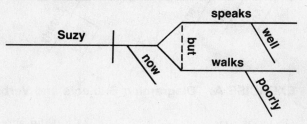

EXERCISE A: Diagraming Compound Subjects and Verbs. Diagram the sentences below.

1. Roses and asters are blooming.

2. They meet and chat.

EXERCISE B: Diagraming Compound Subjects and Verbs with Modifiers. Diagram each sentence below.

1. Several exciting new cars and useful small trucks will be exhibited.

2. They jog daily and race frequently.

3. She smiled and laughed often.

7.9 Diagraming Basic Sentence Parts

Orders, Sentences Beginning with *There* and *Here,* and Interjections

The understood subject *you* is diagramed in the regular subject position, but in parentheses. Interjections, because they have no grammatical relationship to other words, are placed on a short line above the subject.

ORDERS

Wait quietly.

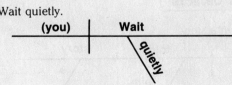

INTERJECTIONS

Gee, I lost quickly.

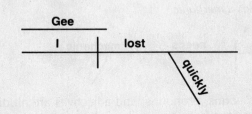

SENTENCES BEGINNING WITH HERE AND THERE

Here at the beginning of a sentence is usually an adverb. It will modify the verb in the sentence. *There* is sometimes used to introduce a sentence. It has no grammatical relation to the rest of the sentence and is diagramed on a short line above the subject.

Here are your tickets.

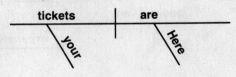

There is one patient waiting.

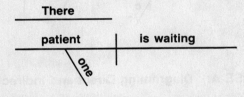

EXERCISE A: Diagraming Orders and Interjections. Diagram the sentences below.

1. Drink slowly.

2. Stand very straight.

3. Hurray, Max has arrived.

EXERCISE B: Diagraming Sentences Beginning with *Here* and *There*. Diagram the sentences below.

1. Here is a very detailed map.

2. There are three girls on the porch.

7.9 Diagraming Basic Sentence Parts

Complements

Direct objects, indirect objects, and subject complements are diagramed in three different ways. A direct object is placed on the same line as the subject and verb. It follows the verb and is separated from it by a short vertical line. A compound direct object is diagramed in a way similar to compound subjects and verbs. The indirect object is placed on a short horizontal line extending from a slanted line drawn directly below the verb. A compound indirect object is diagramed below the verb.

DIRECT OBJECTS

A car needs a *mechanic*.

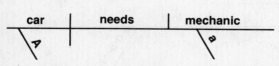

INDIRECT OBJECTS

Ellie told *him* a story.

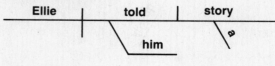

Predicate nouns, pronouns, and adjectives are all diagramed the same way. They are placed after the verb, separated from it by a short slanted line. A compound subject complement is diagramed in the same way as a compound subject or verb.

PREDICATE NOUNS AND PREDICATE ADJECTIVES

Tom was our *captain*.   The house is *white*.   These books are *rare* and *expensive*.

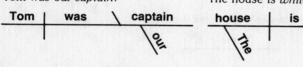   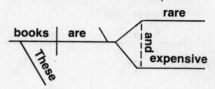

EXERCISE A: Diagraming Direct and Indirect Objects. Diagram the sentences below.

1. Maria made her bed carefully.

2. Joe gave Susan a new flashlight.

EXERCISE B: Diagraming Subject Complements. Diagram the sentences below.

1. The night seems very dark.

2. Her new room was unusually cold.

3. This old document must be historic and very valuable.

8.1 Prepositional Phrases

Prepositional Phrases That Act as Adjectives

A phrase is a group of words, without a subject and verb, that functions in a sentence as a single part of speech. An adjective phrase is a prepositional phrase that modifies a noun or pronoun.

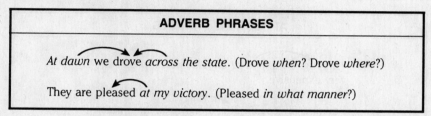

ADJECTIVE PHRASES
The car *with the blue top* is my father's. (*Which* car?)
I rented the room *in the attic*. (*Which* room?)

Prepositional Phrases That Act as Adverbs

An adverb phrase is a prepositional phrase that modifies a verb, adjective, or adverb by pointing out where, when, in what manner, or to what extent.

ADVERB PHRASES
At dawn we drove *across the state*. (Drove *when*? Drove *where*?)
They are pleased *at my victory*. (Pleased *in what manner*?)

EXERCISE A: Identifying Adjective Phrases. Underline each adjective phrase in the sentences below and circle the word it modifies.

EXAMPLE: I bought a (lamp) with a red shade.

1. I ordered a pancake with maple syrup.
2. A book without any illustration may be very interesting.
3. This is the new road to the state park.
4. The sound of the rain on the roof is very loud.
5. Mimi just read a book about Winston Churchill.
6. The winter coat in the closet no longer fits.
7. An investigator uncovered a file of important papers.
8. Strawberries with cream is grandmother's favorite.
9. When did the car in the driveway arrive?
10. I just lost my list of errands.

EXERCISE B: Identifying Adverb Phrases. Underline each adverb phrase and circle the word it modifies.

EXAMPLE: In the breadbox you (will find) three rolls.

1. The heavy snow stopped in the late morning.
2. The teacher was disturbed at Bob's attitude.
3. Without their help we could never have finished the job.
4. The entire trial was completed in two weeks.
5. My parents left for their vacation a week later.
6. At two the post office reopened for business.
7. Foolishly, the fullback charged into Southside's huge line.
8. In a year a new bridge was built.
9. Yes, I certainly am ready for a good lunch.
10. Our basketball team practiced late into the night.

8.2 | Appositives in Phrases

Appositives

An appositive is a noun or pronoun placed next to another noun or pronoun to identify, rename, or explain it.

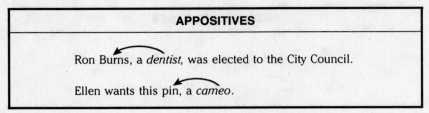

APPOSITIVES
Ron Burns, a *dentist,* was elected to the City Council.
Ellen wants this pin, a *cameo.*

Appositive Phrases

An appositive phrase is an appositive with modifiers. It stands next to a noun or pronoun and adds information or details. Appositives and appositive phrases can also be compound.

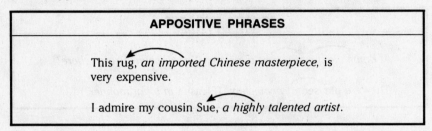

APPOSITIVE PHRASES
This rug, *an imported Chinese masterpiece,* is very expensive.
I admire my cousin Sue, *a highly talented artist.*

EXERCISE A: Identifying Appositives and Appositive Phrases. Underline each appositive or appositive phrase and circle the word it renames.

EXAMPLE: I spoke to Mr. Hartmann, the principal.

1. His favorite team, the Boston Celtics, always seems to win.
2. Sally's essay, a paper on the environment, needs some more work.
3. Your recipe, a favorite of your uncle's, is too rich.
4. I carefully examined the used car, a Plymouth.
5. She reported on the Gilbert Islands, a group of atolls in the Pacific.
6. Mozart, a musical genius, only lived to be thirty-six.
7. We all praised the letter, a magnificent piece of work.
8. Grace Willis, a graphic artist, will lecture to our class.
9. *Citizen Kane,* an early film by Orson Welles, has become a legend.
10. Marie chose her graduation presents, a pearl necklace and a gold watch.

EXERCISE B: Using Appositives and Appositive Phrases in Sentences. Add an appositive or an appositive phrase in the space provided in each sentence.

EXAMPLE: I spoke to Dr. Brown, _a famous surgeon._

1. I think I know Keith, _____.
2. This novel, _____, is well written.
3. She will order her favorite dessert, _____.
4. Washington, D.C., _____, has many hotels.
5. My father, _____, has always been helpful.

8.3 Participles in Phrases

Participles

A participle is a form of a verb that acts as an adjective. There are two kinds of participles: present participles and past participles.

Present Participles	Past Participles
A *smiling* pupil received an award.	I can repair the *broken* watch.
Jogging, he reached a park.	*Finished,* we left for home.

Verb or Participle?

Verb phrases and participles are sometimes confused. When a participle comes after a helping verb it is part of a verb phrase. A participle used as an adjective stands by itself and modifies a noun or pronoun.

Verb Phrases	Participles
A child *was crying.*	I heard a *crying* child.
Bill *has been elected.*	Bill is our *elected* captain.

EXERCISE A: Identifying Present and Past Participles. Underline the participle in each sentence below. If it is a present participle, write *present;* if it is a past participle, write *past.*

EXAMPLE: The <u>waiting</u> bus suddenly left.   ___*present*___

1. Can you find a new reading exercise? _____
2. Mrs. Jones is a paid volunteer. _____
3. Laughing, the boys raced across the court. _____
4. We all agree that this is a growing problem. _____
5. Who is our chosen representative? _____

EXERCISE B: Distinguishing Between Verbs and Participles. Identify each of the underlined words as either a *verb* or *participle.* If the word is a participle, circle the word it modifies.

EXAMPLE: Yes, this is a <u>growing</u> (problem.)   ___*participle*___

1. My uncle has been <u>taken</u> to the hospital. _____
2. The director decided to join the <u>planning</u> board. _____
3. <u>Digging</u>, she found a large metal trunk. _____
4. The <u>scrubbed</u> child looked strangely pale. _____
5. We are <u>going</u> to the concert this weekend. _____
6. The reference book was <u>opened</u> to the final chapter. _____
7. She made a highly <u>praised</u> speech. _____
8. Lewis was carefully <u>pouring</u> oil into the saucepan. _____
9. Bob, a good athlete, has been <u>training</u> daily. _____
10. Have you <u>completed</u> the assignment yet? _____

8.3 Participles in Phrases

Participial Phrases

A participial phrase is a present or past participle that is modified by an adverb or adverb phrase or that has a complement. The entire phrase acts as an adjective in a sentence.

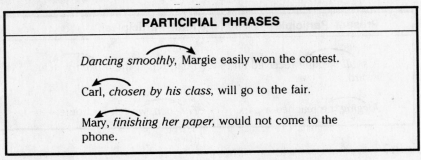

PARTICIPIAL PHRASES

Dancing smoothly, Margie easily won the contest.

Carl, *chosen by his class,* will go to the fair.

Mary, *finishing her paper,* would not come to the phone.

EXERCISE A: Recognizing Participial Phrases. Underline each participial phrase in the sentences below and circle the noun or pronoun it modifies.

EXAMPLE: Driving carefully, we reached the school.

1. The company, paid by mail, failed to deliver the item.
2. Given any excuse, Tommy will tell a joke.
3. The reader, troubled by the article, wrote to the paper.
4. Shouting wildly, the team attacked the goalpost.
5. Collecting stamps for years, Grandfather sold his collection.
6. His money, earned at part-time jobs, helped pay for the trip.
7. Involved in the book, Paul did not hear the bell.
8. Sketching in the background, the artist quickly finished.
9. The horses, placed in a row, kept inching forward.
10. Proceeding slowly, the governor shook everyone's hand.

EXERCISE B: Using Participles in Sentences. Use the following participial phrases in original sentences. Make certain the phrase stands right in front or right after the noun or pronoun it modifies.

EXAMPLE: given a job
    Given a job , Ted always does his best.

1. elected president _____
2. driving cautiously _____
3. asking a question _____
4. involved in the movie _____
5. assisted by a student _____
6. training daily _____
7. broken in half _____
8. urged to explain _____
9. playing her clarinet _____
10. camped in the mountains _____

8.4 Gerunds in Phrases

Gerunds

A gerund is a form of verb that acts as a noun. Gerunds can be used as subjects, direct objects, predicate nouns, and objects of prepositions.

GERUNDS
Swimming is my favorite activity. (*Swimming* is the subject.) I always enjoy *swimming*. (*Swimming* is the direct object.)

Gerund Phrases

A *gerund phrase* is a gerund with modifiers or a complement, all acting together as a noun.

GERUND PHRASES
Swimming every day is a regular activity. (Gerund phrase used as subject.) I enjoy *swimming fast*. (Gerund phrase used as direct object.)

EXERCISE A: Recognizing Gerunds and Gerund Phrases. Underline the gerund or gerund phrase in each sentence. In the space provided tell how it is used.

EXAMPLE: The counselor spoke about <u>smoking</u>. _____*obj. of prep.*_____

1. Working hard is often its own reward. _____

2. My mother always enjoys driving. _____

3. I know people who are obsessed with eating all the time. _____

4. Groping in the dark is not my idea of fun. _____

5. It seems that his favorite activity is sleeping. _____

6. I don't believe in choosing sides. _____

7. Practicing basketball is all Willie does. _____

8. My father's job is managing the New York office. _____

9. Young people used to dream about making movies. _____

10. Yes, I began cleaning my room this morning. _____

EXERCISE B: Using Gerunds and Gerund Phrases in Sentences. Write original sentences that use the gerunds or gerund phrases below.

EXAMPLE: growing tall
    Growing tall is his major goal.

1. driving to school _____

2. making excuses _____

3. laughing _____

4. baking chocolate chip cookies _____

5. cheating _____

8.5 | Infinitives in Phrases

Three Uses of Infinitives

An infinitive is the form of a verb that comes after the word *to* and acts as a noun, adjective, or adverb.

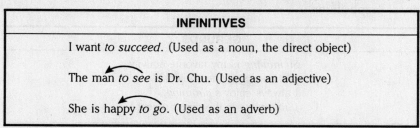

INFINITIVES
I want *to succeed*. (Used as a noun, the direct object)
The man *to see* is Dr. Chu. (Used as an adjective)
She is happy *to go*. (Used as an adverb)

Infinitive Phrases

An infinitive phrase is an infinitive with modifiers or a complement, all working as a single part of speech.

INFINITIVE PHRASES
I want *to succeed in high school*. (Used as a noun, the direct object)
The man *to see today* is Dr. Chu. (Used as an adjective)
She is happy *to go with us*. (Used as an adverb)

EXERCISE A: Recognizing Infinitives and Infinitive Phrases. Underline the infinitive or infinitive phrase in each sentence. In the space provided, tell whether it is used as a noun, adjective, or adverb.

EXAMPLE: To win is not that important.   _noun_

1. Louise decided to go tomorrow. _____
2. Her desire to act is very strong. _____
3. This new novel is easy to read. _____
4. To reach the high school is not that simple. _____
5. We expect to drive to Baltimore. _____
6. They are too lazy to walk to school. _____
7. The place to visit is the Library of Congress. _____
8. Her idea of breakfast is to have a cup of coffee. _____
9. To reach that number is not possible on this phone. _____
10. He had no choice except to go. _____

EXERCISE B: Using Infinitives and Infinitive Phrases in Sentences. Write original sentences that use the infinitives or infinitive phrases below.

EXAMPLE: to wait for friends
        I hate to wait for friends.

1. to buy a stereo _____
2. to talk endlessly _____
3. to practice _____
4. to listen carefully _____
5. to open a window _____

8.6 Diagraming Prepositional Phrases and Appositives

Prepositional Phrases

The diagram for a prepositional phrase is drawn under the word it modifies. The diagram has two parts: a slanted line for the preposition and a horizontal line for the object of the preposition. Adjectives that modify the object are placed beneath the object. The diagram for an adjective phrase is placed directly under the noun or pronoun that the phrase modifies. The diagram for an adverb phrase is placed directly under the verb, adjective, or adverb that the phrase modifies.

ADJECTIVE PHRASES

Your table *in the restaurant* is now ready.

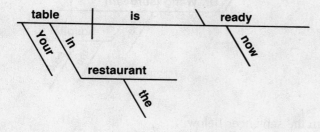

ADVERB PHRASES

My aunt often walks *to our old stately library*.

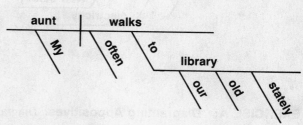

EXERCISE A: Diagraming Adjective Phrases. Diagram the sentences below.

1. The book in the window is quite expensive.

2. I want a room with a beautiful view.

EXERCISE B: Diagraming Adverb Phrases. Diagram the sentences below.

1. Mother frequently drives to our new mall.

2. These old shoes are easier on my tired feet.

3. Sam carefully placed the blue plates on the new table.

8.6 Diagraming Prepositional Phrases and Appositives

Appositives

To diagram an appositive, place it in parentheses next to the noun or pronoun it renames. Any adjectives or adjective phrases that modify the appositive are positioned directly beneath it.

APPOSITIVES

Thomas Edison, *the inventor of electricity*, grew up in New Jersey.

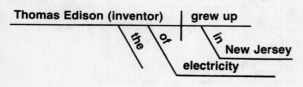

I spoke to Dr. Wang, *the surgeon in the new hospital*.

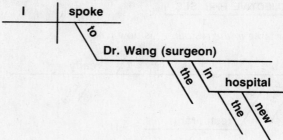

EXERCISE A: Diagraming Appositives. Diagram the sentences below.

1. Mrs. Walters, the principal, addressed the assembly.

2. Tom Chambers, the captain of our football team, resigned.

3. This is Cindy, a true champion.

4. Our coach was Mickey, a warm, friendly, sympathetic person.

EXERCISE B: More Work with Appositives. Diagram the sentences below.

1. I spoke to Dr. Jason, a close friend.

2. I will go to Boston, one of the original colonial cities.

9.1 | Adjective Clause

Recognizing Adjective Clauses

A clause is a group of words with its own subject and verb. An independent clause has a subject and a verb and can stand by itself as a complete sentence. A subordinate clause has a subject and a verb but cannot stand by itself in a sentence. It is only part of a sentence. An *adjective clause* is a subordinate clause that modifies a noun or pronoun. Adjective clauses answer the questions *What kind?* or *Which one?* Most adjective clauses begin with one of the relative pronouns: *that, which, who, whom,* and *whose.* They can also begin with such words as *when, since,* or *where.*

ADJECTIVE CLAUSES

This is the statue *that he wrote about.*

The girl *whom we chose* is on the honor roll.

In the days *since the accident occurred* the family has remained indoors.

EXERCISE A: Identifying Adjective Clauses. Underline the adjective clause in each sentence and circle the word it modifies.

EXAMPLE: The (ring) that you ordered is not available.

1. This is a day that we will all remember.
2. A painting which everyone dislikes was removed from the hall.
3. He is a man who someday may be our governor.
4. The Korean War, which dragged on for three long years, finally ended in 1953.
5. There was a time when I drove to the country each summer.
6. Fritz Kreisler, the famous violinist who was a child prodigy, also studied medicine and art.
7. The girl whose wallet I found has been absent for a week.
8. Cracow, which is also spelled Krakow, is a city in Poland.
9. Have you met the candidate whom he wants to nominate?
10. We have had three responses in the time since we placed the advertisement.

EXERCISE B: Writing Sentences with Adjective Clauses. Add an adjective clause in each sentence below.

EXAMPLE: The book ___that I need now___ was taken from the library.

1. This is the house _____.
2. The teacher whom _____ just resigned.
3. Do you know the girl _____?
4. The report _____ is not accurate.
5. Here is a musician _____.
6. The president _____ is George Washington.
7. A teacher whose _____ was Mrs. Gordon.
8. I know a doctor _____.
9. This is the book _____.
10. She remembers the store _____.

9.1 Adjective Clauses

Combining Sentences with Adjective Clauses

Two sentences sometimes can be combined into one by changing one of them into an adjective clause. Such a combination is particularly useful when the information in both sentences is closely related.

COMBINING SENTENCES
Dr. Samuel Mudd set the broken leg of Lincoln's assassin. He was later sentenced to life imprisonment for this act.
Dr. Samuel Mudd, *who set the broken leg of Lincoln's assassin*, was later sentenced to life imprisonment for this act.

EXERCISE A: Combining Sentences with Adjective Clauses. Each item below contains two sentences. Change one of them into an adjective clause and include it in the other sentence. You may change some words.

EXAMPLE: Enrico Caruso is considered the greatest operatic tenor of all time. He made his New York debut in 1903.

Enrico Caruso, ___who made his New York debut in 1903___, is considered the greatest operatic tenor of all time.

1. Bill Bradley is a United States Senator from New Jersey. He once was an outstanding basketball player with the New York Knicks.

_____

_____

2. Casablanca is a port city in Morocco. President Roosevelt and Prime Minister Winston Churchill met there in 1943.

_____

_____

3. Castor oil is pressed from the castor bean. It is used for brake fluid, paints, and as a general lubricant.

_____

_____

EXERCISE B: Combining More Sentences with Adjective Clauses. Follow the directions in Exercise A.

1. The Organization of American States (OAS) helps promote economic progress in the Americas. It was organized in 1948.

_____

_____

2. Soho is a district in West London in Great Britain. It is noted for its Italian and French restaurants.

_____

_____

9.2 Adverb Clauses

Recognizing Adverb Clauses

An adverb clause is a subordinate clause that modifies a verb, an adjective, or an adverb. Adverb clauses begin with subordinate conjunctions such as *as, although, since, when, if,* and *because*. Adverb clauses tell when, where, how, why, or to what extent.

ADVERB CLAUSES
Chuck cannot go *since he has not finished his chores*.
Because she has been ill, Lisa takes a nap every day.
This trick is easier *when you practice it for a while*.
The book ends better *than I expected*.

EXERCISE A: Identifying Adverb Clauses. Underline the adverb clause in each sentence. Circle the verb, adjective, or adverb it modifies.

EXAMPLE: I (came) because I was asked.

1. If the roads are sanded, we will leave immediately.
2. I am often tired after I work a six-day week.
3. His new idea sounds as if it might actually work.
4. My haircut and shampoo took longer than I had imagined.
5. Whenever I visit a museum, I greatly enjoy the exhibits.
6. Her apartment will be brighter when she repaints it.
7. Wait where I can signal you from the window.
8. Because he lied in court, his sentence was longer.
9. My brother was upset when I phoned from the station.
10. While you wait, the artist will complete your portrait.

EXERCISE B: Writing Sentences with Adverb Clauses. Add an adverb clause in each sentence below.

EXAMPLE: _____When I get your message_____ , I will leave.

1. I will not make any plans _____.
2. _____, Bill has been unable to work.
3. Your job will be easier_____.
4. Mom will pick up your photos _____.
5. My class lasted longer_____.
6. I will finish my homework early_____.
7. _____, your room will look neater.
8. _____, the teacher will consider changing your grade.
9. As soon as my aunt phoned from Los Angeles, _____
_____.
10. I was much happier_____.

9.2 Adverb Clauses

Elliptical Adverb Clauses

In certain adverb clauses, words are left out. These clauses are said to be elliptical. In an elliptical adverb clause, the verb or the subject and verb are understood rather than actually stated.

ELLIPTICAL ADVERB CLAUSES	
Elliptical	**Completely Written Out**
Mark is older *than Bill*.	Mark is older *than Bill (is old.)*
My parents gave more to him *than to me*.	My parents gave more to him *than (they gave) to me.*
My sister is as tall *as I*.	My sister is as tall *as I (am tall)*.

EXERCISE A: Recognizing Elliptical Clauses. Underline each elliptical clause in the sentences below. In the space provided write out the rest of the missing clause.

EXAMPLE: My roast is better <u>than his</u>.   *roast is*

1. His explanation is just as likely as yours. _____

2. Lucy can run faster than Bill. _____

3. I think I understand him better than she. _____

4. Are they as lonely as I? _____

5. Our neighbors are much richer than we. _____

6. I know Barbara better than her. _____

7. The other team members were as angry as I. _____

8. Hank is always much later than Fred. _____

9. The guest spoke more to her than to me. _____

10. Do you think you are happier than she? _____

EXERCISE B: Writing Sentences Using Elliptical Clauses. Use the elliptical clauses below in original sentences.

EXAMPLE: as humorous as I
          My friends say that Bobby is as humorous as I.

1. than my father _____

2. as friendly as she _____

3. than they _____

4. as my friends _____

5. than she and I _____

6. hungrier than anyone else _____

7. than to me _____

8. more than she _____

9. as restless as he _____

10. than the principal _____

9.3 | Classifying Sentences by Structure

The Simple Sentence

A simple sentence consists of a single independent clause. It must contain a subject and verb. Some simple sentences contain various compounds—a compound subject or a compound verb or both.

SIMPLE SENTENCES
This <u>book</u> <u>is</u> unusually interesting.
My <u>brother</u> and <u>sister</u> <u>will arrive</u> tomorrow.
<u>He</u> <u>opened</u> the package and <u>found</u> a new camera.

The Compound Sentence

A compound sentence consists of two or more independent clauses. The independent clauses in a compound sentence are joined by a comma and one of the coordinating conjunctions: *and, but, nor, for, or, so, yet*. The two independent clauses can also be joined with a semicolon (;).

COMPOUND SENTENCES
This <u>book</u> <u>is</u> unusually interesting, and <u>I</u> <u>will finish</u> it tonight.
My <u>brother</u> <u>will arrive</u> tomorrow, but my <u>sister</u> <u>will</u> not <u>come</u> until Sunday.
<u>He</u> <u>opened</u> the package; <u>it</u> <u>contained</u> a new camera.

EXERCISE A: Examining Simple Sentences. Each sentence below is a simple sentence. Underline all the subjects once and all the verbs twice.

EXAMPLE: Both <u>bridges</u> <u>are</u> under water and <u>will</u> not <u>open</u>.

1. The trains and the buses recently changed their schedules.
2. We reached the second traffic light and turned left.
3. Have you found the map to Albany yet?
4. Bill and Sue opened their gifts and examined them carefully.
5. Almost every afternoon my grandfather takes a nap.

EXERCISE B: Examining Compound Sentences. Each sentence below is a compound sentence. Underline each subject once and each verb twice.

EXAMPLE: The <u>bridge</u> <u>is</u> down; <u>all</u> of the roads <u>have been closed</u>.

1. The situation is confusing, but I hope to have more news soon.
2. I hope to do better this year, and I am going to study regularly.
3. Movies are just great, but I still enjoy a good book often.
4. I have twenty record albums; my brother has many more.
5. Tom and Steve will meet us at the game, or they will phone their regrets.

9.3 | Classifying Sentences by Structure

The Complex Sentence

A complex sentence consists of one independent clause and one or more subordinate clauses. The subordinate clause can be an adjective or adverb clause.

COMPLEX SENTENCES

INDEPENDENT CLAUSE   SUBORDINATE CLAUSE
This is the film projector (that he wants to buy).

SUBORDINATE CLAUSE   INDEPENDENT CLAUSE
(If I visit the county fair,) *I will bring you something*.

The Compound-Complex Sentence

A compound-complex sentence consists of two or more independent clauses and one or more subordinate clauses.

COMPOUND-COMPLEX SENTENCES

SUBORDINATE CLAUSE   INDEPENDENT CLAUSE
(If I am asked to play first-string,) *it will be an important*

INDEP. CLAUSE   SUBORDINATE CLAUSE
milestone for me, but *I am also afraid* (that the challenge
will be too great.)

EXERCISE A: Recognizing Complex and Compound-Complex Sentences. Label each sentence *complex* or *compound-complex*. Underline each independent clause and put parentheses around each subordinate clause.

EXAMPLE: <u>The house</u> (that you described) <u>is too large</u>.   _____*complex*_____

1. As soon as I got the letter, I read the instructions, and I knew that I wanted to go. _____

2. This is the book that Margo wants for her birthday. _____

3. I will help you plan the picnic, which, unfortunately, I will not be able to attend. _____

4. I know the way to the state capital, but I may get lost as we get close since I really have been there only once. _____

5. The company which contacted us on the phone happens to have a bad reputation. _____

EXERCISE B: More Work with Complex and Compound-Complex Sentences. Follow the directions for Exercise A.

1. Although I studied my notes carefully, I still did poorly on the test. _____

2. I can reach my father on the phone, or I will go to his office if I have enough time. _____

3. Is this the tie that father really wants? _____

4. When I get to London, I will buy you a present, but I can't really promise since I may be very busy. _____

5. I like to play my stereo, or I listen to my radio, whenever I have the time. _____

9.4 | Diagraming Clauses

Compound Sentences

To diagram a compound sentence, begin by diagraming each clause separately, one above the other. Then join the clauses at the verbs using a dotted line shaped like a step. Place the conjunction or semicolon on the horizontal part of the step.

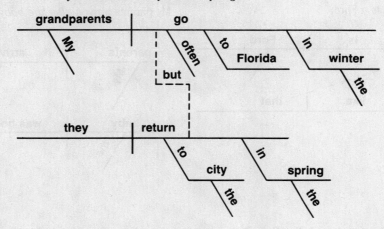

COMPOUND SENTENCE

INDEPENDENT CLAUSE
My grandparents often go to Florida in the winter, but

INDEPENDENT CLAUSE
they return to the city in late spring.

EXERCISE A: Diagraming Compound Sentences. Diagram the sentences below.

1. I opened the door to my bedroom, and I found a present on my bed.

2. This is our first visit; we have never been to Chicago before.

EXERCISE B: More Diagraming Compound Sentences. Diagram the sentences below.

1. Myra would not agree to our plan, but she later changed her mind.

2. I know the way to Boston; I will probably become lost in certain parts of the city.

9.4 Diagraming Clauses

Subordinate Clauses

A complex sentence contains one independent clause and one or more subordinate clauses. In a diagram of a complex sentence, each clause is placed on a separate horizontal line. A subordinate adjective clause is placed on a horizontal line of its own beneath the independent clause. The two clauses are then connected by a dotted line from the noun or pronoun being modified to the relative pronoun in the adjective clause. A subordinate adverb clause is also written on a horizontal line of its own beneath the independent clause. The subordinate conjunction is written along a dotted line. This line extends from the modified word in the independent clause to the verb in the adverb clause.

ADJECTIVE CLAUSES	ADVERB CLAUSES

The car *that you like* is a Ford.

My parents arrived *after the baby was born*.

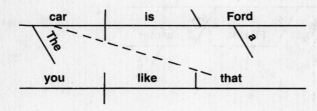

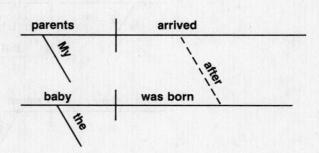

EXERCISE A: Diagraming Adjective Clauses. Diagram the sentences below.

1. The book which you borrowed from the library is in our own bookcase.

2. This is the movie that we saw in Los Angeles.

EXERCISE B: Diagraming Adverb Clauses. Diagram the sentences below.

1. If you buy that typewriter, you can use my spare ribbons.

2. The next bus leaves whenever it is filled with passengers.

10.1 Avoiding Fragments

Recognizing Fragments

A fragment is a group of words that does not express a complete thought. It is only part of a sentence. Any group of words that cannot stand alone is a fragment.

Fragments	Complete Sentences
at the football game	We met at the football game.
should have arrived there	My family should have arrived there.
a woman in a yellow dress	A woman in a yellow dress asked to see you.
when I received the letter	When I received the letter, I answered immediately.

EXERCISE A: **Recognizing Fragments.** Label each fragment *F* and each sentence *S*.

EXAMPLE: Since you expect an answer now. ___F___

1. Would be able to go tomorrow. _____
2. If I can remember the directions to her house. _____
3. We can leave at once. _____
4. At the end of the first half. _____
5. A group of boys charging down the path. _____
6. When we spoke to them on the phone yesterday. _____
7. The arrangements have been made in advance. _____
8. In spite of all their objections. _____
9. Have not charged full price for this album. _____
10. Everyone planned to meet at the pizza parlor. _____

EXERCISE B: **Recognizing More Fragments.** Follow the directions in Exercise A.

1. On the morning of the big game. _____
2. There was an accident at the railroad station. _____
3. A bus racing toward the intersection. _____
4. Although he invited me to the party. _____
5. Must be out of the apartment by this time tomorrow. _____
6. I know the way to the downtown shopping area. _____
7. The book with the World War II pictures. _____
8. After trying to convince them all morning. _____
9. Chewing gum is not permitted in our school. _____
10. At another time, perhaps in another era. _____

10.1 Avoiding Fragments

Phrase Fragments

There are four kinds of phrases—prepositional, participial, gerund, and infinitive. Phrases should not be capitalized and punctuated as if they were sentences.

PHRASE FRAGMENTS
near the old television
smiling to the crowd

Clause Fragments

Adjective and adverb clauses are not complete sentences although they have subjects and verbs. These subordinate clauses should not be capitalized as if they were sentences.

CLAUSE FRAGMENTS
if they want to do something foolish
that I wanted to buy

EXERCISE A: Changing Phrase Fragments into Sentences. Use each of the phrase fragments below anywhere in a complete sentence. You must add a *subject* and a *verb*.

EXAMPLE: under the staircase
             Under the staircase I found my skates.

1. in half an hour _____

2. between you and me _____

3. changing my clothes _____

4. to reach the station _____

5. smoking cigarettes _____

6. of another kind _____

7. growing different vegetables _____

8. with all her friends _____

9. to open my present _____

10. told to report to the principal _____

EXERCISE B: Changing Clause Fragments into Sentences. Use each clause fragment below in a complete sentence. You must add a complete *independent clause* with another subject and verb.

EXAMPLE: that I need
             The file that I need is on a shelf.

1. if I get his message _____

2. whom she asked _____

3. because I like them _____

4. which Bill wants _____

5. whose wallet I found _____

6. since you chose to go _____

7. until the new family moved in _____

8. who was in the room _____

9. that I found there _____

10. whenever I write _____

10.2 Avoiding Run-ons

Two Kinds of Run-ons

A run-on is two or more complete sentences that are not properly joined or separated. One kind consists of two sentences that are not joined or separated by any punctuation at all. Another kind consists of two sentences punctuated only with a comma.

RUN-ONS	
With No Punctuation	**With Only a Comma**
A trip to a state park seemed like a good idea everyone agreed to go next Sunday.	The aroma from the oven was overwhelming, I opened the stove door and saw a large tray of chocolate-chip cookies.

EXERCISE A: Recognizing Run-ons. Some of the sentences are complete sentences; others are run-ons. Write S if the item is a complete sentence and RO if the item is a run-on.

EXAMPLE: I inflated the bike tire, it wouldn't hold the air. ___RO___

1. Jakob Grimm and his brother Wilhelm collected German folk tales, they were later published and became famous as *Grimm's Fairy Tales*. _____

2. People in this area like to talk about the great flood water that covered the entire downtown shopping center and many other parts of the town. _____

3. She opens her mail every day; she pays her bills every week. _____

4. Jute is a tropical plant grown primarily for its fiber, it is used to make burlap, twine, and backing yarns for rugs. _____

5. Juneau is the state capital of Alaska it has an airport, an ice-free harbor, and a seaplane base. _____

EXERCISE B: More Work with Run-ons. Follow the same directions as above.

1. Paso Robles in southern California is a resort city that features hot springs. _____

2. Rhinoceroses have thick skin and feature one or two nasal horns, there are both black and white types. _____

3. Rhubarb is a plant whose leaf blades are poisonous it also has fleshy leaf-stalks that are used to make delicious pies and sauces. _____

4. The Rhine, an 820-mile river in Europe, is used by freighters to transport coal, iron, and grain. _____

5. Sir Walter Scott was a famous British writer and poet, among his famous works were *Ivanhoe*, *Kenilworth*, and *The Bride of Lammermoor*. _____

10.2 Avoiding Run-ons

Three Ways to Correct Run-ons

There are three ways to correct a run-on—using an end mark, using a comma and a coordinating conjunction, or using a semicolon.

THREE WAYS TO CORRECT A RUN-ON	
Run-on	Leonard Bernstein is a famous American conductor you probably know him best as the composer of *West Side Story*.
Method	**Corrected Run-on**
End mark— period (.) question (?)	Leonard Bernstein is a famous American conductor. You probably know him best as the composer of *West Side Story*.
A comma and a coordinating conj. (,but)	Leonard Bernstein is a famous American conductor, but you probably know him best as the composer of *West Side Story*.
A semicolon (;)	Leonard Bernstein is a famous American conductor; you probably know him best as the composer of *West Side Story*.

EXERCISE A: Correcting Run-ons. Each sentence below is a run-on. On a separate sheet of paper, rewrite each run-on using one of the three methods of correction shown above. Vary your methods.

1. Howard Pyle writes stories of adventure and chivalry, he is the author of *The Merry Adventures of Robin Hood of Great Renown*.
2. Nebraska was admitted to the union in 1867 as the 37th state today it is an important agricultural state in which corn, wheat, and sorghum are grown.
3. Our hockey team ended the season with a heart-breaking loss, the players cleaned out their lockers quickly and left for home.
4. Thomas Masaryk was the chief founder and first president of Czechoslovakia in 1948 he was pushed from a window to his death, or he committed suicide.
5. We must have a complete physical examination each year before practicing any sport in fact the coach won't allow anyone on the field without a medical clearance.

EXERCISE B: Correcting More Run-ons. Follow the directions in Exercise A.

1. The city of Paterson, New Jersey, was founded by Alexander Hamilton in 1791, early it was a center of the textile industry with both cotton-spinning mills and silk manufacturing.
2. My family has not decided what to do about moving, we may either rent an apartment in town or try to buy another house.
3. The shamrock is a plant with leaves of three leaflets for some time it has been the emblem of Ireland.
4. Shallots are used by many chefs in cooking they are similar to the onion but not quite as strong in flavor.
5. Gilbert Stuart was the most famous American painter of his day, he is best known today for his three portraits of George Washington.

10.3 | Avoiding Misplaced Modifiers

Recognizing Misplaced Modifiers

When modifiers, phrases and clauses that act as adjectives or adverbs, are placed too far from the words they modify, confusion can result. A modifier should be placed as close as possible to the word it modifies. A modifier that is placed incorrectly is called a misplaced modifier.

Misplaced Modifiers	Corrected
I often eat fish in a restaurant *with french fries*. *While waiting at the station*, her ticket was lost.	I often eat fish *with french fries* at a restaurant. *While waiting at the station*, she lost her ticket.

EXERCISE A: Recognizing Misplaced Modifiers. Some of the sentences below are correct; others contain misplaced modifiers. If the sentence is correct, write C. If the sentence contains a misplaced modifier, write MM.

EXAMPLE: Having phoned my parents, the bus began to pull out. ___MM___

1. After staying out late, the house was hard to find. _____
2. The statue was destroyed in the storm erected in 1869. _____
3. Changing into my jeans, I began to work in the garden. _____
4. Flying near the airport, the cars looked like small beetles. _____
5. The dinner prepared by a chef was allowed to spoil. _____
6. Skating on the frozen canal, my ankles began to swell. _____
7. Racing to the gate, I greeted my Uncle Bill. _____
8. The speaker was late chosen to go first. _____
9. To get this free offer, a phone call must be made. _____
10. To get a refund, you must send in a coupon. _____

EXERCISE B: Recognizing More Misplaced Modifiers. Follow the directions in Exercise A.

1. Bill counted the days waiting for Christmas. _____
2. The room is too expensive with a view of the lake. _____
3. Opening the envelope, Joan found her lost identification card. _____
4. Walking through the lobby, grandfather's beard almost touched the floor. _____
5. The graphic is missing designed by the famous artist. _____
6. The wall around the city needs to be repaired. _____
7. Examining his shoe, Bob saw a hole on the bottom. _____
8. To prepare the stew, the potatoes should be cut in cubes. _____
9. Thinking very hard, Edward finally found the answer. _____
10. To clean brass, you should use a soft cloth. _____

10.3 Avoiding Misplaced Modifiers

Correcting Misplaced Modifiers

Three kinds of modifiers are commonly misplaced—prepositional phrases, participial phrases, and adjective clauses. Misplaced modifiers are corrected by placing the modifier as close as possible to the word it modifies.

Misplaced Modifier	Corrected
The art critic found a painting in an abandoned warehouse *that had been missing for fifty years*.	The art critic found a painting *that had been missing for fifty years* in an abandoned warehouse.

EXERCISE A: Correcting Misplaced Modifiers. Each sentence below contains a misplaced modifier. Rewrite the sentence by moving the modifier close to the word it modifies. You may change words if necessary.

EXAMPLE: Rushing toward the accident victim, his body was covered with a blanket.
            Rushing toward the accident victim, I covered his body with a blanket.

1. Smiling at the rock singer, his autograph was given to me.

   _____

2. A movie began the film festival that won an Academy Award.

   _____

3. Reaching the box office, the concert tickets were sold out.

   _____

4. To begin a research project, the card catalog should be checked first.

   _____

5. The batter hit a home run who had been in a terrible slump.

   _____

EXERCISE B: Correcting More Misplaced Modifiers. Follow the directions in Exercise A.

1. My mother usually makes spaghetti from her own recipe with meatballs.

   _____

2. Climbing the stairs slowly, the fifth floor was finally reached.

   _____

3. I looked in the textbook for the meaning of the word with the glossary.

   _____

4. The fare to the city is too expensive that he wants to visit.

   _____

5. Running down in his pajamas, his shame wouldn't let him open the door.

   _____

   _____

11.1 Two Levels of Standard English

Formal English

Formal English uses traditional standards of correctness. It often has complex sentence structures and uses a wide vocabulary.

WRITING FORMAL ENGLISH

1. Contractions should not be used.
2. Slang is never used.
3. The pronoun *you* should not be used in a general way to refer to "a person."
4. Correct grammatical structures and precise wording should be used.

Informal English

Informal English is conversational in tone. It uses a smaller vocabulary and shorter sentences than formal English.

WRITING INFORMAL ENGLISH

1. Contractions are acceptable.
2. Popular expressions are acceptable if they are not overused.
3. The pronoun *you* may be used in a general way.
4. Sentences may be loose and conversational.

EXERCISE A: Recognizing Formal and Informal English. Label each sentence below *F* (formal) or *I* (informal).

EXAMPLE: Instead of planning the party carefully, Juanita decided to play it by ear. ___*I*___

1. You don't have to cook in a fancy way to cook well. _____

2. In pre-Columbian times, some Plains Indians were nomadic. _____

3. Advertisements purport to inform consumers; they actually address the consumers' hidden feelings. _____

4. Ralph was overwhelmed by the pretentiousness of the other guests at the party. _____

5. The cursor shows you where the next letter you type will appear. _____

6. Wendy couldn't make it to the party because she was sicker than a dog. _____

7. Roger's behavior really ticked Julie off. _____

8. Some readers resort to literature not to find out the truth about life but to escape from it. _____

9. You have to practice to do this trick successfully. _____

10. Perennials are plants that annually produce flowers and seed from the same root structure.

EXERCISE B: Using Formal English. Rewrite the five informal sentences you identified in Exercise A using formal English.

EXAMPLE: *Instead of planning the party carefully, Mary decided to improvise as circumstances dictated.*

1. _____

2. _____

3. _____

4. _____

5. _____

12.1 The Principal Parts of Verbs

Regular Verbs

Every verb has four principal parts: the present, the present participle, the past, and the past participle. Regular verbs form the past and past participle by adding -ed or -d to the present form.

PRINCIPAL PARTS OF REGULAR VERBS			
Present	**Present Participle**	**Past**	**Past Participle**
look	(am) looking	looked	(have) looked
inform	(am) informing	informed	(have) informed
move	(am) moving	moved	(have) moved
use	(am) using	used	(have) used

In sentences the four principal parts are used alone or with helping verbs.

SENTENCES USING THE PRINCIPAL PARTS OF *CALL*
Present: I *call* my aunt every week.
Present Participle: I *am calling* Dr. Johnson this morning.
Past: She *called* to invite me to a party.
Past Participle: He *has called* three different stores.

EXERCISE A: Identifying the Principal Parts of Regular Verbs. Underline the verb or verb phrase in each sentence. Then identify the principal part used to form the verb.

EXAMPLE: We <u>watched</u> the tennis match. ___*past*___

1. I write a column for the school newspaper. _____
2. Gary waited half an hour for the bus. _____
3. Karen is visiting her relatives in Iowa. _____
4. Are you listening to the explanation? _____
5. The speaker had paused for a moment. _____
6. They were wearing their basketball uniforms. _____
7. Mr. Kelly coached the football team last season. _____
8. Amy had remembered to pack a flashlight. _____
9. We are planning a number of surprises. _____
10. These musicians usually play some contemporary music. _____

EXERCISE B: Using Principal Parts of Regular Verbs. Write the form of the verb in parentheses that correctly completes the sentence.

EXAMPLE: We are (begin) the project tomorrow. ___*beginning*___

1. Kevin has (live) in Kentucky all his life. _____
2. The players were (discuss) their strategies. _____
3. I still (exercise) every day. _____
4. We have (agree) to meet at 7 P.M. _____
5. Before he spoke, the entertainer (smile) at the audience. _____
6. Frank had already (perform) his act before I arrived. _____
7. He is (attempt) to run a four-minute mile. _____
8. Yesterday Jennifer (promise) she would join our group. _____
9. Kenneth is (practice) a new song on his clarinet. _____
10. I am (suggest) that you make several changes. _____

12.1 The Principal Parts of Verbs

Irregular Verbs

An irregular verb does not form the past and past participle by adding *-ed* or *-d* to the present form. Irregular forms must be memorized.

PRINCIPAL PARTS OF SOME IRREGULAR VERBS			
Present	**Past Participle**	**Past**	**Past Participle**
be	(am) being	was	(have) been
bring	(am) bringing	brought	(have) brought
burst	(am) bursting	burst	(have) burst
choose	(am) choosing	chose	(have) chosen
cost	(am) costing	cost	(have) cost
drink	(am) drinking	drank	(have) drunk
fly	(am) flying	flew	(have) flown
grow	(am) growing	grew	(have) grown
pay	(am) paying	paid	(have) paid
rise	(am) rising	rose	(have) risen
swear	(am) swearing	swore	(have) sworn
swim	(am) swimming	swam	(have) swum
teach	(am) teaching	taught	(have) taught
throw	(am) throwing	threw	(have) thrown
write	(am) writing	wrote	(have) written

EXERCISE A: Supplying the Principal Parts of Irregular Verbs. Fill in the missing principal parts in the exercise below.

EXAMPLE: _drive_ _____   _driving_ _____   drove _____   _driven_ _____

1. _____ _____ swore _____ _____
2. pay _____ _____ _____
3. _____ being _____ _____ _____
4. _____ _____ _____ cost _____
5. write _____ _____ _____
6. _____ bringing _____ _____ _____
7. _____ _____ _____ risen _____
8. _____ _____ chose _____ _____
9. burst _____ _____ _____
10. _____ _____ threw _____ _____

EXERCISE B: Using the Principal Parts of Irregular Verbs. Fill in the blanks with the correct verb form from the choices shown in parentheses.

EXAMPLE: Angela   _threw_   the ball to first base.   (threw, throwed)

1. Edward had never _____ so far before.   (swam, swum)
2. My grandmother _____ me how to bake bread. (taught, teached)
3. Last summer I _____ to California. (flied, flew)
4. We have _____ all the juice in the refrigerator. (drank, drunk)
5. I have already _____ two inches this year. (grown, grew)

12.2 The Six Tenses of Verbs

The Basic Forms of the Six Tenses

Tenses are verb forms that indicate time of action or state of being. Each of the six tenses has a basic form. All basic forms are derived from three principal parts: the present, the past, and the past participle.

Tense	Basic Form of *Take*	Principal Part Used
Present	I take	Present
Past	I took	Past
Future	I will take	Present
Present Perfect	I have taken	Past Participle
Past Perfect	I had taken	Past Participle
Future Perfect	I will have taken	Past Participle

Conjugating the Basic Forms of Verbs

A conjugation is a list of the singular and plural forms of a verb in a particular tense. A short conjugation shows the forms of a verb used with one personal pronoun. Note that the verb forms used with *he* are also used with *she* and *it,* and the verb forms used with *we* are also used with *you* and *they.*

BASIC FORMS OF *SEE*			
Tense	With *I*	With *he*	With *we*
Present	I see	he sees	we see
Past	I saw	he saw	we saw
Future	I will see	he will see	we will see
Present Perfect	I have seen	he has seen	we have seen
Past Perfect	I had seen	he had seen	we had seen
Future Perfect	I will have seen	he will have seen	we will have seen

EXERCISE A: Recognizing Basic Forms and Tense. Underline the verb or verb phrase in each sentence. Then write the tense of the verb on the line to the right.

EXAMPLE: We <u>will</u> <u>have</u> <u>completed</u> the training program by next fall.   ___*future perfect*___

1. She will attend a conference in Washington, D.C. _____

2. Barbara and Marie refused to sign the petition. _____

3. The dancers rehearse every day. _____

4. We had considered several alternative plans. _____

5. I have memorized two poems by Walt Whitman. _____

EXERCISE B: Conjugating Basic Forms. Complete both of the short conjugations below. Use the pronouns shown in parentheses.

EXAMPLE:

want (with *she*)   1. visit (with *he*)   2. say (with *they*)

___she wants___   _____   _____

___she wanted___   _____   _____

___she will want___   _____   _____

___she has wanted___   _____   _____

___she had wanted___   _____   _____

___she will have wanted___   _____   _____

12.3 The Progressive Forms of Verbs

Recognizing Progressive Forms

Each of the six tenses has a progressive form. The six progressive forms of a verb make use of one principal part: the present participle.

THE PROGRESSIVE FORMS OF *WRITE*		
Tense	**Progressive Form**	**Principal Part Used**
Present	I am writing	
Past	I was writing	
Future	I will be writing	The Present
Present Perfect	I have been writing	Participle
Past Perfect	I had been writing	
Future Perfect	I will have been writing	

Conjugating the Progressive Forms of Verbs

To conjugate the progressive forms of a verb, add the present participle of a verb to a conjugation of the basic forms of *be*. Below are progressive forms of the verb *try* used with two different pronouns.

THE PROGRESSIVE FORMS OF *TRY*		
Tense	**With *I***	**With *she***
Present	I am trying	she is trying
Past	I was trying	she was trying
Future	I will be trying	she will be trying
Present Perfect	I have been trying	she has been trying
Past Perfect	I had been trying	she had been trying
Future Perfect	I will have been trying	she will have been trying

EXERCISE A: Recognizing Progressive Forms and Tenses. Each sentence below contains a verb in its progressive form. Underline the verb phrase in each sentence. Then write the tense of that verb phrase on the line at the right.

EXAMPLE: She had been studying all afternoon.   *past perfect*

1. The workers will be repairing the building. _____

2. The architect is explaining his plans. _____

3. Susan will have been working for two hours by 9 a.m. _____

4. They were discussing important political issues. _____

5. Diane has been telling us a folk tale. _____

EXERCISE B: Conjugating Progressive Forms. Complete a short conjugation of the progressive forms of each verb listed below. Use the pronouns shown in parentheses.

EXAMPLE: buy (with *you*)   1. study (with *I*)   2. watch (with *he*)

you are buying   _____   _____

you were buying   _____   _____

you will be buying   _____   _____

you have been buying   _____   _____

you had been buying   _____   _____

you will have been buying   _____   _____

12.4 Active and Passive Voice

Two Voices

Most verbs have two voices—the active and the passive. A verb is active when its subject performs the action. A verb is passive when its subject does not perform the action.

TWO VOICES	
Active Voice	**Passive Voice**
Kenneth *completed* the job.	The job *was completed* by Kenneth.
Ann *interviewed* the artist.	The artist *was interviewed* by Ann.

Forming the Tenses of Passive Verbs

A passive verb is made from a form of *be* plus a past participle.

THE PASSIVE FORMS OF THE VERB *SAVE*	
Tense	**Passive Form**
Present	it is saved
Past	it was saved
Future	it will be saved
Present Perfect	it has been saved
Past Perfect	it had been saved
Future Perfect	it will have been saved

EXERCISE A: Distinguishing Between Active and Passive Voice. On the line at the right identify the verb in each sentence as active or passive.

EXAMPLE: These flowers were grown by my neighbor. ___*passive*___

1. Peter built this model airplane. _____

2. The blue ceramic bowl was purchased by Arlene. _____

3. The chaotic scene was described by an eyewitness. _____

4. The decorator removed the painting from the wall. _____

5. A well-informed guide led us through the museum. _____

6. This event will be remembered for a long time. _____

7. Harvey took pictures of the graduation ceremony. _____

8. An amusing anecdote was told to me by my nephew. _____

9. The new student was introduced to the class. _____

10. Francis raced towards the crowd of people. _____

EXERCISE B: Conjugating Verbs in the Passive Voice. Complete a short conjugation of the verbs below in the passive voice. Use the pronouns indicated in parentheses.

EXAMPLE: find (with *it*)	1. ask (with *he*)	2. change (with *it*)
it is found	_____	_____
it was found	_____	_____
it will be found	_____	_____
it has been found	_____	_____
it had been found	_____	_____
it will have been found	_____	_____

12.4 Active and Passive Voice

Using Active and Passive Voices

Use the active voice whenever possible. Use the passive voice to emphasize the receiver of an action or to point out the receiver whenever the performer is unknown, unimportant, or not named in the sentence.

USES OF THE ACTIVE AND PASSIVE VOICES

The touchdown *was scored* by Martin. (Wordy and weak passive; better as active voice: Martin *scored* the touchdown.)
Mayor Johnson *was honored* by his colleagues. (Correct passive; emphasizes Mayor Johnson, the receiver of the action.)
We *were told* to leave the building at once. (Correct passive; the performer is not named in the sentence.)

EXERCISE A: Using Verbs in the Active Voice. Rewrite each sentence below, changing the verb from passive voice to active voice. Make any necessary word changes.

EXAMPLE: New computers were recently purchased by our school.
        Our school recently purchased new computers.

1. The awards were presented by the principal.

   _____

2. During the first act, a solo was performed by Gloria.

   _____

3. Our trip to Tucson, Arizona, was planned by Russell and John.

   _____

4. A hole in one was shot by Louis on his first try.

   _____

5. An important speech was made by the president.

   _____

6. A number of pictures have been drawn by me since my arrival.

   _____

7. A bright red cap was worn by Harriet.

   _____

8. A large record collection is shared by the members of my family.

   _____

9. I have been asked by Mr. Peterson to prepare a short speech.

   _____

10. You will be trained by an experienced craftsman.

   _____

EXERCISE B: Avoiding Unnecessary Uses of the Passive Tense. Rewrite the sentences in the following paragraph. Change passive verbs to active ones to improve the paragraph. Use a separate sheet of paper.

EXAMPLE: The Jamestown settlers were helped by Native Americans.
        Native Americans helped the Jamestown settlers.

   (1) The colony of Jamestown was settled by the English in 1607. (2) One hundred and four men and boys had been sent by a group of merchants in England. (3) The settlers had been instructed by their sponsors to look for gold and other valuables. (4) They were also told by the merchants to find a route to Asia. (5) A difficult beginning was experienced by these early settlers, but eventually they prospered.

12.5 Glossary of Troublesome Verbs

Troublesome Verbs

Study the principal parts of troublesome verbs. Learn to distinguish between the meanings of confusing pairs of verbs.

INFORMATION ABOUT TROUBLESOME VERBS

1. *Ain't:* Avoid using *ain't* in both writing and speaking.
2. *Burst:* The present, past, and past participle of burst are all *burst*. Bust and *busted* are incorrect.
3. *Did and Done: Did* is used alone as a main verb. *Done* requires a helping verb such as *have* or *has*.
4. *Dragged and Drug: Drag* is a regular verb. *Drug* is not one of its principal parts.
5. *Drowned and Drownded:* The past and past participle of *drown* is *drowned*. *Drownded* is incorrect.
6. *Gone and Went: Gone* is the past participle of the verb *go*. *Gone* requires a helping verb such as *have* or *has*. *Went* is the past of *go* and is never used with a helping verb.
7. *Have and Of:* Do not use *of* in place of the helping verb *have*.
8. *Lay and Lie: Lay* means "to put" or "to place." It is followed by a direct object. *Lie* means "to rest in a reclining position" or "to be situated." It is never followed by a direct object.
9. *Learn and Teach: Learn* means "to receive knowledge." *Teach* means "to give knowledge."
10. *Leave and Let: Leave* means "to allow to remain." *Let* means "to permit."

EXERCISE A: Using Troublesome Verbs Correctly. Circle the verb in the parentheses that correctly completes each sentence.

EXAMPLE: We had (went, (gone)) to the park with Karen.

1. We (ain't, aren't) ready to begin.
2. Have you (dragged, drug) this scarf through the mud?
3. The lifeguard saved the swimmer before she (drownded, drowned).
4. I could (of, have) listened to that music for hours.
5. Where have I (laid, lay) my briefcase?
6. When the balloon (busted, burst), I was startled.
7. I want Cindy to (learn, teach) me how to make a quilt.
8. The cost of living has (risen, raised) sharply.
9. (Let, Leave) me finish what I am doing.
10. Joseph (did, done) his homework before dinner.

EXERCISE B: Using Troublesome Verbs in Sentences. Use each verb listed below in a sentence.

EXAMPLE: sneaked
    The burglars sneaked through the empty house.

1. burst _____
2. drowned _____
3. did _____
4. done _____
5. dragged _____
6. gone _____
7. went _____
8. have _____
9. lay _____
10. learn _____

13.1 Cases of Personal Pronouns

Three Cases

The relation between a pronoun's form and its use in a sentence is known as case. English has three cases: nominative, objective, and possessive.

THE THREE CASES OF PERSONAL PRONOUNS		
Case	**Pronoun Forms**	**Uses in Sentences**
Nominative	I, we; you; he, she, it, they	Subject of a Verb Predicate Pronoun
Objective	me, us; you; him, her, it, them	Direct Object Indirect Object Object of a Preposition
Possessive	my, mine, our, ours; your, yours, his, her, hers, its, their, theirs	To Show Ownership

EXERCISE A: Determining Case. On the lines at the right write the case of the underlined personal pronoun in each sentence below.

EXAMPLE: <u>They</u> urged Louise to accept the job. _____nominative_____

1. It was <u>I</u> who delivered the message. _____
2. The members of the club elected <u>him</u> president. _____
3. Is this jacket <u>yours</u>? _____
4. <u>She</u> redecorated the room. _____
5. Please show <u>us</u> the letter. _____
6. A woman with a large hat sat in front of <u>me</u>. _____
7. The person in charge is <u>he</u>. _____
8. <u>Their</u> home is in Indiana. _____
9. <u>Mine</u> is the umbrella with the blue handle. _____
10. The orchestra played a song for <u>them</u>. _____

EXERCISE B: Identifying Case and Use. Write the case of each underlined pronoun. Then write its use.

EXAMPLE: <u>He</u> met the new instructor. _____nominative_____ _____subject of a verb_____

1. The blue sedan is <u>ours</u>. _____ _____
2. <u>They</u> made an important announcement. _____ _____
3. Madeline showed <u>me</u> the photograph. _____ _____
4. Neil recognized <u>them</u> immediately. _____ _____
5. <u>His</u> ideas are quite original. _____ _____
6. The first speaker will be <u>she</u>. _____ _____
7. Sandra sat down beside <u>me</u>. _____ _____
8. Donna lent Jane <u>her</u> suitcase. _____ _____
9. Rachel and <u>I</u> played tennis yesterday. _____ _____
10. Patrick sent Bill and <u>me</u> tickets to the show. _____ _____

13.1 Cases of Personal Pronouns

The Nominative Case

Use a personal pronoun in the nominative case (1) as the subject of a verb or (2) as a predicate pronoun.

USES OF THE NOMINATIVE CASE	
Subject of a Verb	*They* are expecting a package.
	After school Ralph and *he* headed for home.
Predicate Pronoun	The chairperson will be *she*.

The Objective Case

Use a personal pronoun in the objective case as (1) a direct object, (2) an indirect object, or (3) the object of a preposition.

USES OF THE OBJECTIVE CASE	
Direct Object	I admire *him*.
	Deborah met Tom and *her* in the gym.
Indirect Object	The usher handed *them* a program.
Object of a Preposition	Alice sat beside *her*.
	Do not leave without Michael and *me*.

EXERCISE A: Using Nominative Pronouns. Fill in each blank with a nominative pronoun. Then write how the pronoun is used in the sentence.

EXAMPLE: ___You___ can accompany me to the museum. ___subject of a verb___

1. Since this morning, _____ has been reading. _____
2. Henry and _____ took a walk together. _____
3. The most outstanding dancer in the class is _____. _____
4. Carefully, _____ moved the priceless antique statue. _____
5. According to the plan, _____ will meet in Chicago. _____
6. The scientist who made the discovery is _____. _____
7. It was _____ who answered the telephone. _____
8. The Robinsons and _____ vacationed in Colorado. _____
9. The losers will probably be John and _____. _____
10. The film reviewers are Nancy and _____. _____

EXERCISE B: Using Objective Pronouns. Fill in each blank with an objective pronoun. Then write how the pronoun is used in the sentence.

EXAMPLE: A friend introduced ___us___. ___direct object___

1. I have not seen _____ for a long time. _____
2. We enjoy having people around _____. _____
3. The speaker's arguments convinced _____. _____
4. Alexandra showed _____ her latest drawings. _____
5. The younger children sat in front of _____. _____
6. The artist painted _____ a picture. _____
7. During the conference, we sat opposite _____. _____
8. The hostess thanked _____ for the gift. _____
9. Daniel wrote _____ a note last week. _____
10. Carol is playing against _____ in the semifinals. _____

13.1 Cases of Personal Pronouns

The Possessive Case

Use the possessive case of personal pronouns before nouns to show possession. Use certain personal pronouns by themselves to indicate possession. Personal pronouns in the possessive case are never written with apostrophes.

USES OF THE POSSESSIVE CASE	
Before Nouns	*His* brother plays the clarinet.
	Can you come to *our* house?
By Themselves	*Mine* is the gray suitcase.
	Is that notebook *yours*?

EXERCISE A: Using Possessive Pronouns. Circle the correct word from the choices in parentheses.

EXAMPLE: (Their's, (Theirs)) are the skis in the corner.

1. Is (your's, yours) the gray cap on the sofa?
2. The kitten was playing with (its, it's) favorite toy.
3. (Hers, Her's) was an exceptionally interesting childhood.
4. I always enjoy (you, your) Sunday dinners.
5. Thomas brought (his, his') radio to the beach.
6. (It's, Its) too early to know for sure.
7. One of (me, my) favorite movies is on television tonight.
8. This store claims that (their's, theirs) are the lowest prices.
9. (They're, Their) first business venture was a great success.
10. The final decision is (your's, yours).

EXERCISE B: Using the Three Cases of Personal Pronouns. Circle the correct word from the choices in parentheses.

EXAMPLE: The senator and ((he,) him) spoke to the committee.

1. It must have been (them, they) who sent me this gift.
2. We expect Barbara and (he, him) to arrive shortly.
3. Grace and (me, I) explored the area.
4. No one listened to Donald and (me, I).
5. The composer of the song I am playing is (he, him).
6. (Their's, Theirs) is a productive collaboration.
7. Can the hotel accommodate them and (us, we)?
8. The Turners and (we, us) went to the theater.
9. The dog wagged (it's, its) tail as his master appeared.
10. The attorney asked Eugene and (me, I) some questions.

13.2 Cases of *Who* and *Whom*

Separate Uses in Sentences

Who is a pronoun in the nominative case. Like other nominative pronouns, *who* is used as the subject of a verb.

USING *WHO*	
The Subject of a Question	*Who* finished first?
The Subject of a Subordinate Clause	I met the woman *who* directs the recreation program here.

Whom is a pronoun in the objective case. Like other objective pronouns, *whom* is used (1) as the direct object of a verb or (2) as the object of a preposition.

USING *WHOM*	
The Direct Object of a Verb	*Whom* did she ask to return?
	It was William *whom* they interviewed.
The Object of a Preposition	To *whom* shall I address this note?
	Here is the artist about *whom* I was speaking.

EXERCISE A: Using *Who* and *Whom*. Write *who* or *whom* in each blank below.

EXAMPLE: Ronald, after ___*whom*___ do I speak?

1. Beside _____ are you sitting?

2. Have you met the pilot _____ is flying the plane?

3. For _____ are we waiting?

4. The actor _____ the critics selected received an award.

5. Tell me the name of the congressman _____ you are describing.

6. You recommended _____ for the job?

7. _____ drew this cartoon?

8. Everyone _____ we spoke with agreed with us.

9. Woody Allen is the filmmaker _____ he most admires.

10. _____ has traveled through the most states?

EXERCISE B: Choosing the Correct Form and Use of *Who* and *Whom*. Circle the correct form of the pronoun in parentheses. Then write the number that describes how the pronoun is used in the sentence: 1 (subject of a question); 2 (subject of a subordinate clause); 3 (direct object of a verb); 4 (object of a preposition).

EXAMPLE: She is the author ((who) whom) wrote this novel. ___2___

1. (Who, Whom) received the most votes? _____

2. (Who, Whom) have they nominated for secretary? _____

3. With (who, whom) are you having lunch? _____

4. Michael is the runner (who, whom) came in first. _____

5. (Who, Whom) besides you can't find his notebook? _____

6. John was the person (who, whom) they sent to California. _____

7. Mary is the one (who, whom) represents us on the student council. _____

8. (Who, Whom) in the first act has the most lines? _____

9. I photographed the man (who, whom) works with my father. _____

10. Alan is the person to (who, whom) he dedicated his first book. _____

14.1 Agreement Between Subjects and Verbs

The Number of Nouns and Pronouns

Nouns and pronouns have number. They are either singular, indicating one, or plural, indicating more than one.

NOUNS AND PRONOUNS		
Part of Speech	**Singular**	**Plural**
Nouns	mountain	mountains
	tax	taxes
	mouse	mice
Personal Pronouns	I, me, my, mine	we, us, our, ours
	you, your, yours	you, your, yours
	he, him, his, she, her, it, its	they, them, their, theirs
Indefinite Pronouns	anybody, each, nobody	both, few, many

The Number of Verbs

Verbs also have number. Subjects and verbs must agree in number. Third-person singular verb forms in the present tense change to show number. The third-person singular form adds an -s, or -es. Forms of the verb *be* also change to show number.

VERBS	
Singular	*First and Second Person:* (I, you) begin
	Third Person: (he, she, it) begins
Plural	*First, Second, and Third Person:* (we, you, they) begin

EXERCISE A: Identifying the Number of Nouns and Pronouns. Label each of the following words as *singular* or *plural*.

EXAMPLE: cities _____*plural*_____

1. home _____
2. he _____
3. ranches _____
4. we _____
5. nobody _____
6. several _____
7. women _____
8. everyone _____
9. it _____
10. acres _____
11. railroads _____
12. I _____
13. she _____
14. desert _____
15. they _____
16. others _____
17. oxen _____
18. something _____
19. children _____
20. lunches _____

EXERCISE B: Identifying the Number of Verbs. Underline the present tense verb in the parentheses that agrees with the subject in each sentence. Then label the verb as *singular* or *plural*.

EXAMPLE: He (<u>teaches</u>, teach) science. _____*singular*_____

1. They (enjoy, enjoys) singing. _____
2. A dog (bark, barks) loudly. _____
3. Our guests (arrives, arrive) shortly. _____
4. Plants (grow, grows) slowly. _____
5. I (was, were) happy on my birthday. _____

14.1 Agreement Between Subjects and Verbs

Agreement with Singular and Plural Subjects

A singular subject requires a singular verb. A plural subject requires a plural verb.

AGREEMENT BETWEEN SUBJECTS AND VERBS	
Singular	**Plural**
Our <u>car</u> usually <u>starts</u> easily.	The <u>students</u> <u>play</u> basketball on Thursdays.
Jean <u>collects</u> antique furniture.	According to the newspaper, <u>leaders</u> <u>are meeting</u> in Washington.

When a prepositional phrase comes between a subject and its verb, it does not affect subject-verb agreement.

A PREPOSITIONAL PHRASE SEPARATING A SUBJECT AND ITS VERB
That <u>book</u> of riddles <u>amuses</u> me.
The <u>magazines</u> on this shelf <u>belong</u> to me.

EXERCISE A: Recognizing Subject-Verb Agreement. Underline the subject of each sentence once. Then select the verb in parentheses that agrees with this subject and underline it twice.

EXAMPLE: The <u>customers</u> on the long line (<u>wait</u>, waits) patiently.

1. A delivery of eggs (arrive, arrives) early each morning.
2. The cafeteria (open, opens) at noon.
3. The tree near the tulips (shade, shades) the porch.
4. That old train station (looks, look) very familiar.
5. My aunt usually (send, sends) me a picture post card when she travels.
6. The invitations to the party (is, are) ready to send.
7. The children (walk, walks) to the meadow each day.
8. The people on the crowded street (rush, rushes) home.
9. Our weekly meetings (begin, begins) at 7:30 p.m.
10. The animals in the show (belong, belongs) to members of our club.

EXERCISE B: Selecting Verbs that Agree with Singular and Plural Subjects. For each sentence, underline the verb in parentheses that agrees with the subject. Then label the sentence *S* if the subject is singular and *P* if the subject is plural.

EXAMPLE: The chairs in the auditorium (is, <u>are</u>) new.   _P_

1. The members of the committee (speaks, speak) to us today. _____
2. The barn across from the stables (belong, belongs) to us. _____
3. Several men (assist, assists) us in the shop. _____
4. A cabinet filled with trophies (stand, stands) in the corner. _____
5. The tourists on the bus (admire, admires) the scenery. _____
6. The paintings along this wall (is, are) family portraits. _____
7. His idea really (interest, interests) me. _____
8. His plans to travel to Peru (sound, sounds) exciting. _____
9. The houses along the shore (is, are) vacant now. _____
10. The designer of all this clothing (live, lives) in Paris. _____

14.1 Agreement Between Subjects and Verbs

Agreement with Compound Subjects

Two or more singular subjects joined by *or* or *nor* require a singular verb. However, if one part of a compound subject joined by *or* or *nor* is singular and the other part is plural, the verb agrees with the closest subject.

COMPOUND SUBJECTS JOINED BY *OR* OR *NOR*	
Two Singular Subjects	<u>Vivian</u> or <u>Mark</u> <u>writes</u> the editorial.
	Neither <u>Carl</u> nor <u>Eve</u> <u>remembers</u> his name.
One Singular and One Plural Subject	Neither the <u>coach</u> nor the <u>players</u> <u>are</u> here.
	Neither the <u>players</u> nor the <u>coach</u> <u>is</u> here.

A compound subject joined by *and* requires a plural verb. The only exceptions are (1) when the parts of the subject are considered one thing or (2) when the subject is modified by *each* or *every*.

COMPOUND SUBJECTS JOINED BY *AND*
<u>Spring</u> and <u>summer</u> <u>are</u> my favorite seasons.
<u>Macaroni</u> and <u>cheese</u> <u>is</u> on the menu.
Each <u>boy</u> and <u>girl</u> <u>receives</u> a souvenir.

EXERCISE A: Using Compound Subjects Joined by *Or* or *Nor*. Underline the the verb in parentheses that agrees with the subject of each sentence.

EXAMPLE: Either Ann or Ted (<u>inspects</u>, inspect) the equipment.

1. Even though it is late, neither Evan nor Betty (is, are) here.
2. Either the students or their teacher (conduct, conducts) the debate.
3. Neither the lifeguard nor the swimmers (stay, stays) here all day.
4. A salad or two vegetables (comes, come) with your dinner.
5. Either the salespeople or the manager (demonstrate, demonstrates) the equipment.
6. Neither my parents nor Dianne (agrees, agree) with me.
7. Either the librarian or her assistant (is, are) available to help.
8. Neither the trainees nor their instructor (uses, use) shortcuts.
9. It is possible that the lawyer or his client (is, are) mistaken.
10. Neither the fruit juice nor the sandwiches (is, are) ready.

EXERCISE B: Using Compound Subjects Joined by *And*. Underline the verb in parentheses that agrees with the subject of each sentence.

EXAMPLE: Marcia and her colleagues (<u>give</u>, gives) their report today.

1. Each volunteer and contributor (receives, receive) an invitation.
2. The governor and the senator (discuss, discusses) political issues.
3. Spaghetti and meatballs (was, were) served for lunch.
4. Both Carla and Brian (agree, agrees) that more planning is needed.
5. Every record and book (is, are) on sale today.
6. The costumes and props (belong, belongs) backstage.
7. The Hendersons and their niece (go, goes) skiing every winter.
8. Bacon and eggs (is, are) my favorite breakfast.
9. Mr. Gordon and his boss (have, has) offices on this floor.
10. Each flower and bush (is, are) carefully tended.

14.2 Special Problems with Subject-Verb Agreement

Agreement in Sentences with Unusual Word Order

When a subject follows a verb, they still must agree in number.

SENTENCES WITH INVERTED WORD ORDER
In this envelope <u>are</u> several newspaper <u>clippings</u>. There <u>were</u> two <u>letters</u> on my desk. Here <u>are</u> the <u>photographs</u> I took at the beach. Where <u>are</u> the <u>tickets</u> to the concert?

Agreement with Indefinite Pronouns

An indefinite pronoun used as a subject must agree with its verb. Some indefinite subjects are always singular. Other indefinite pronouns are always plural. Still other indefinite pronouns can be either singular or plural depending on the number of the pronoun's antecedent.

INDEFINITE PRONOUNS						
Always Singular			**Always Plural**		**Singular or Plural**	
anyone	somebody	each	both	many	all	most
everybody	someone	no one	few	others	any	none
everything	something	one			more	some

EXERCISE A: Recognizing Subject-Verb Agreement in Sentence with Inverted Word Order. Underline the subject in each sentence. Then circle the verb in parentheses that agrees with it.

EXAMPLE: Across from the park ((stand,) stands) the <u>buses</u>.

1. Inside this box (is, are) important papers.
2. There (was, were) many paintings on the walls.
3. When (is, are) the next Giants game?
4. Along the winding roads (walk, walks) the traveler.
5. Around the corner (is, are) a new boutique.
6. Here (is, are) four samples I want you to examine.
7. What (is, are) the names of the senators on the committee?
8. Who (is, are) the leading candidate for governor?
9. There (is, are) the elevator that goes to the top floor.
10. Here on the left (is, are) the horse I usually ride.

EXERCISE B: Making Indefinite Pronouns and Verbs Agree. Underline the verb in parentheses that best completes each sentence.

EXAMPLE: No one (<u>expects</u>, expect) this warm weather to last.

1. Each of the problems (was, were) solved.
2. Few of the participants (remember, remembers) the incident.
3. All of his pets (demand, demands) a great deal of attention.
4. Everything stated in these reports (appears, appear) to be correct.
5. Both of the writers (agree, agrees) that we need to make changes.

14.3 Agreement Between Pronouns and Antecedents

Making Personal Pronouns and Antecedents Agree

A personal pronoun must agree with its antecedent in person and number. Avoid shifts in person. Never use *you* to refer to the person you are writing about. Avoid shifts in number. Use a singular personal pronoun to refer to two or more singular antecedents joined by *or* or *nor*.

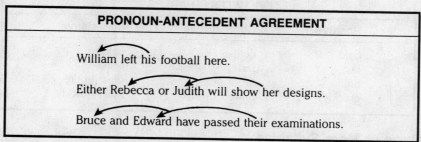

PRONOUN-ANTECEDENT AGREEMENT

William left his football here.

Either Rebecca or Judith will show her designs.

Bruce and Edward have passed their examinations.

Agreement Between Personal Pronouns and Indefinite Pronouns

Use a singular personal pronoun when the antecedent is a singular indefinite pronoun.

AGREEMENT WITH INDEFINITE PRONOUNS

Each of the actors supplies his own costume.

Take one of these forms and mail it back to me.

Neither of the automobiles is in its correct spot.

EXERCISE A: Writing Personal Pronouns That Agree with Antecedents. Complete each sentence with an appropriate personal pronoun.

EXAMPLE: After they read the poem, Sue and Ann returned to ___*their*___ seats.

1. Either Mary or Ellen will lend you _____ camera.
2. The doctor and his wife signed _____ names to the petition.
3. Neither Stephen or James remembered to bring _____ football.
4. The desk has a calendar and a pencil sharpener on _____.
5. The cat, awakened by the noise, opened _____ eyes.
6. My parents want me to write to _____ often while I am away.
7. Gabriel said _____ had never seen such an exciting movie.
8. The girls explored the area on _____ bicycles.
9. Margaret explained why _____ decided to study Latin.
10. Kenneth welcomed _____ cousins when they arrived.

EXERCISE B: Choosing Personal Pronouns That Agree with Indefinite Pronouns. Underline the pronoun in parentheses that correctly completes each sentence below.

EXAMPLE: Ask anyone in this group to show you (their, <u>her</u>) notes.

1. Everyone on the committee completed (his, their) research.
2. Both of the generals are in (his, their) uniforms.
3. See if either of the girls wants (her, their) lesson now.
4. No one in the Computer Users' Club has returned (his, their) survey.
5. Everything in the museum is in (its, their) proper place.

15.1 Regular Adjectives and Adverbs

Modifiers of One or Two Syllables

Adjectives and adverbs have three degrees of comparison: positive, comparative, and superlative. Use *-er* or *more* to form the comparative degree and *-est* and *most* to form the superlative degree.

DEGREES OF COMPARISON—MODIFIERS OF ONE OR TWO SYLLABLES		
Positive	**Comparative**	**Superlative**
cold	colder	coldest
fast	faster	fastest
polite	more polite	most polite
quickly	more quickly	most quickly

Modifiers of Three or More Syllables

Use *more* and *most* to form the comparative and superlative degrees of modifiers of three or more syllables.

DEGREES OF COMPARISON—MODIFIERS OF THREE OR MORE SYLLABLES		
Positive	**Comparative**	**Superlative**
beautiful	more beautiful	most beautiful
carefully	more carefully	most carefully

EXERCISE A: Recognizing the Three Degrees of Comparison. Identify the degree of comparison of each underlined modifier by writing P for positive, C for comparative, or S for superlative on the line.

EXAMPLE: Margaret is <u>older</u> than I am. ___C___

1. Gregory is the <u>fastest</u> of all the runners here. _____

2. Louise felt <u>tired</u>. _____

3. These letters arrived <u>sooner</u> than I expected. _____

4. Donald is <u>more conscientious</u> about his work than he used to be. _____

5. I <u>slowly</u> removed the lid. _____

6. Then the <u>most unexpected</u> thing happened. _____

7. This jewel is <u>more precious</u> than that one. _____

8. The lecture hall is <u>larger</u> than the lounge. _____

9. I pedaled <u>furiously</u> up the hill. _____

10. He is the <u>most intelligent</u> person I know. _____

EXERCISE B: Forming the Comparative and Superlative Degrees of Regular Modifiers. Fill in the chart below by writing the comparative and superlative degrees of each modifier. Whenever possible, use the *-er* and *-est* forms.

EXAMPLE: casual   *more casual*   *most casual*

1. long   _____   _____

2. fine   _____   _____

3. foolish   _____   _____

4. neat   _____   _____

5. sympathetic   _____   _____

15.2 Irregular Adjectives and Adverbs

Irregular Modifiers

Learn the irregular comparative and superlative forms of adjectives and adverbs.

DEGREES OF COMPARISON—IRREGULAR MODIFIERS		
Positive	**Comparative**	**Superlative**
bad	worse	worst
badly	worse	worst
far (distance)	farther	farthest
far (extent)	further	furthest
good	better	best
well	better	best
many	more	most
much	more	most

EXERCISE A: Using the Comparative and Superlative Forms of Irregular Modifiers. Fill in each blank with the correct form of the modifier in parentheses.

EXAMPLE: This is the ___best___ story I have ever written.   (good)

1. I feel _____ today than I did yesterday.   (bad)

2. Ellen spends _____ time practicing the piano than I do.   (much)

3. Of all my friends, Joseph lives the _____ from my house.   (far)

4. I did _____ than Julia on the exam.   (well)

5. Justin is a _____ swimmer than his brother.   (good)

6. That is the _____ colorful flower in the shop.   (much)

7. I will not tolerate a _____ delay.   (far)

8. The team played _____ today than they did last week.   (badly)

9. This is the _____ news I have heard all day.   (good)

10. Ted scored the _____ points of his career this season.   (many)

EXERCISE B: Using Irregular Modifiers in Sentences. Use each word listed below in a sentence. Follow the directions as to which degree of comparison to use.

EXAMPLE: good—comparative degree
   Tina draws better than I do.

1. bad—comparative degree

_____

2. far (distance)—superlative

_____

3. badly—comparative

_____

4. good—superlative

_____

5. well—comparative

_____

15.3 Using Comparative and Superlative Degrees

Comparative and Superlative Degrees

Use the comparative degree to compare two people, places, or things. Use the superlative degree to compare three or more people, places, or things. Avoid double comparisons. Do not use -er and more or -est and most.

USING THE COMPARATIVE DEGREE
Alexander is two years *older* than his brother.
This novel has *fewer* pages than that one.
Catherine is *more interested* in sports than I am.

USING THE SUPERLATIVE DEGREE
Here is the *latest* edition of our newspaper.
Of all my friends, Joyce is the *most patient*.
I think New York is the *most exciting* city of all.

EXERCISE A: Using the Comparative and Superlative Degrees. Underline the correct comparative or superlative form in each sentence.

EXAMPLE: The meeting was the (longer, <u>longest</u>) one we ever had.

1. The first exercise is the (simpler, simplest) of the two.
2. Helen is the (better, best) violinist in our school.
3. This antique is (older, oldest) than any other in my collection.
4. Justine has been waiting the (longer, longest) of all.
5. When I began dancing, I was much (clumsier, clumsiest) than Susan.
6. Lancaster is the (closer, closest) of the two locations.
7. John is the (wealthiest, wealthier) of his four brothers.
8. Theirs is the (larger, largest) of all the houses on this block.
9. It is (sunnier, sunniest) this week than it was last week.
10. It is obvious that Robert is the (taller, tallest) of the twins.

EXERCISE B: Correcting Sentences with Incorrectly Formed Comparisons. On the line after each sentence write the comparative or superlative form that will correct the underlined errors.

EXAMPLE: She is the <u>most popular</u> of the two candidates. _*more popular*_

1. Of the two hotels, this one is the <u>most luxurious</u>. _____
2. This is the <u>most hardest</u> job I have ever had. _____
3. Yours seems to be the <u>best</u> of the two ideas. _____
4. I am feeling <u>more better</u> now that I have had some rest. _____
5. Which of the three sisters is <u>the more athletic</u>? _____
6. We are hoping we can do <u>more better</u> in the next tournament. _____
7. Steven lives <u>more farther</u> from the school than I do. _____
8. I am not certain which of these four hills is the <u>steeper</u>. _____
9. Of all the jokes he told, the last one was the <u>most funniest</u>. _____
10. Conditions here are <u>more worse</u> than they were a year ago. _____

15.4 Making Logical Comparisons

Balanced Comparisons

Compare only items of a similar kind.

CORRECTING UNBALANCED COMPARISONS	
Unbalanced	**Balanced**
My essay is longer than *Nora*. *His tennis racket* is heavier than *the instructor*.	*My essay* is longer than *Nora's essay*. *His tennis racket* is heavier than *the instructor's tennis racket*.

Other and *Else* in Comparisons

When comparing one of a group with the rest of the group, use the word *other* or *else*.

USING *OTHER* OR *ELSE*	
Incorrect	**Correct**
Patrick has attended *more* meetings *than any* club member.	Patrick has attended *more* meetings *than any other* club member.
My father reads *more than anyone* in our family.	My father reads *more than anyone else* in our family.

EXERCISE A: Writing Balanced Comparisons. Rewrite each sentence below, correcting each unbalanced comparison.

EXAMPLE: Andrea's notes are neater than Michael.
 Andrea's notes are neater than Michael's notes.

1. George's diagram is more exact than Henry.

_____

2. Charles's directions are as simple to follow as Randy.

_____

3. Martin's computer has more memory than Philip.

_____

4. My math teacher's tests are longer than my English teacher.

_____

EXERCISE B: Forming Comparisons with *Other* or *Else*. Rewrite each sentence adding *other* or *else* to make the comparison clear.

EXAMPLE: My sister Eva likes to ski more than anyone in our family.
 My sister Eva likes to ski more than anyone else in our family.

1. Mayor Powell gives more speeches than any city politician.

_____

2. I like to play baseball more than any sport.

_____

3. Detective Harris has solved more cases than any investigator.

_____

4. Dr. Parker is more popular than any physician on our staff.

_____

15.5 Glossary of Troublesome Adjectives and Adverbs

Troublesome Adjectives and Adverbs

Learn how to use troublesome modifiers.

TROUBLESOME MODIFIERS		
Word	**Part of Speech**	**Example**
bad	adjective	I felt *bad* when I heard the news.
badly	adverb	She performed *badly* during the audition.
fewer	adjective	This beverage has *fewer* calories.
less	adjective	They asked us to make *less* noise.
good	adjective	Bill has *good* ideas.
well	adjective	I didn't feel *well* this morning.
	or adverb	Betsy swims *well*.
just	adverb	Pour me *just* half a cup of juice.

EXERCISE A: Using Troublesome Adjectives and Adverbs. Underline the word in parentheses that correctly completes each sentence.

EXAMPLE: This stew tastes extremely (<u>good</u>, well).

1. Carol draws (good, well).
2. This milk tastes (bad, badly).
3. I play tennis (bad, badly).
4. There were (fewer, less) people on line an hour ago.
5. The bread you are baking smells (good, well).
6. Although he is out of the hospital, he still doesn't feel (good, well).
7. I eat (less, fewer) sugar than I used to.
8. Why are you reading with (fewer, less) expression?
9. The orchestra played (bad, badly).
10. The first part of your speech sounds (good, well).

EXERCISE B: Using Troublesome Modifiers in Sentences. Use each word listed below as a modifier in an original sentence.

EXAMPLE: less
          This machine uses less energy than our older model.

1. fewer

_____

2. badly

_____

3. good

_____

4. well

_____

5. bad

_____

16.1 Double Negatives

The Mistaken Use of Double Negatives

Do not write sentences with double negatives.

AVOIDING DOUBLE NEGATIVES	
Double Negative	Corrected Sentence
I ca*n't* *never* remember his name.	I can *never* remember his name. I ca*n't* ever remember his name.
They have*n't* given me *none*.	They have given me *none*. They have*n't* given me any.
We *never* saw *no* lions.	We *never* saw any lions. We saw *no* lions.

EXERCISE A: Avoiding Double Negatives in Sentences. Underline the word in parentheses that completes each sentence correctly.

EXAMPLE: I haven't (never, <u>ever</u>) been to Japan.

1. Our group (will, won't) never be able to finish on time.
2. He didn't say (nothing, anything) about his future plans.
3. I (do, don't) want to see anything on television this evening.
4. Nobody had heard (nothing, anything) about the speech.
5. My sister doesn't (ever, never) get up early on weekends.
6. The chairman hasn't appointed (no one, anyone) to head the committee.
7. He (should, shouldn't) never have expected everyone to assist him.
8. She hasn't (ever, never) explained why she is studying this area.
9. We (could, couldn't) see nothing from where we sat.
10. She won't lend me (none, any) of her books.

EXERCISE B: Correcting Sentences with Double Negatives. Rewrite each sentence below in two different ways.

EXAMPLE: I haven't never been to Cape Cod.
<u>*I have never been to Cape Cod.*</u>
<u>*I haven't ever been to Cape Cod.*</u>

1. Don't do nothing until you receive further instructions.

_____

_____

2. There isn't nobody on our team who plays as well as James.

_____

_____

3. William can't find none of the original drafts of his story.

_____

_____

4. They couldn't determine no cause for such an action.

_____

_____

5. They won't allow no one in until 7:45 P.M.

_____

_____

16.2 Twenty Common Usage Problems

Usage Problems

Note the following words and expressions that cause usage problems. Some usage problems occur because two or more words have similar spellings or meanings. Other usage problems occur because the word or words are inappropriate and should be eliminated.

USAGE PROBLEMS
Words with Similar Spellings or Meanings

accept and *except*	*farther* and *further*
advice and *advise*	*in* and *into*
affect and *effect*	*than* and *then*
all ready and *already*	*that, which,* and *who*
among and *between*	*their, there,* and *they're*
beside and *besides*	*to, too,* and *two*

Words or Expressions to Avoid	
at (after *where*)	*due to the fact that*
because (after *the reason*)	*kind of, sort of*
different than	*this here* (omit *here*)
like (before a subject and a verb)	*that there* (omit *there*)

EXERCISE A: Recognizing Correct Usage. Underline the word in parentheses that correctly completes each sentence.

EXAMPLE: The lawyer gave his client some (<u>advice</u>, advise).

1. Terry has (all ready, already) signed us for swimming lessons.
2. This story is quite (different from, different than) your last one.
3. We will discuss this issue (further, farther) at another time.
4. Alan is the candidate (which, who) I supported for class president.
5. Everyone (accept, except) John agrees with the decision.
6. (Their, They're) all waiting for a bus.
7. Valerie goes to the movies more often (than, then) I do.
8. (Due to the fact that, Since) our plane was delayed, we were late.
9. Divide these souvenirs (among, between) the three children.
10. What (affect, effect) does diet have on a person's health?

EXERCISE B: More Practice Recognizing Correct Usage. Underline the word in parentheses that correctly completes each sentence.

EXAMPLE: Henry decided to (<u>accept</u>, except) the invitation to the party.

1. I am looking for it, but I don't know exactly where (it's at, it is).
2. Jennifer was (too, to) tired to watch the late movie.
3. First I read several sources, and (then, than) I planned my report.
4. (This here, This) coat is on sale.
5. The reason I am happy (is, is because) I won the contest.
6. (Their, there) comments were very funny.
7. I moved the desk (in, into) the corner of the room.
8. The results were (sort of, rather) startling.
9. It rained during the afternoon just (like, as) you predicted.
10. Will anyone (beside, besides) Eileen help with the decorations?

17.1 Capitals for First Words

Sentences

Capitalize the first word in declarative, interrogative, imperative, and exclamatory sentences.

SENTENCES
Declarative: She is losing the race. *Interrogative:* Where is the milk? *Imperative:* Bring me that pen. *Exclamatory:* What a surprise you gave me!

Quotations

Capitalize the first word in a quotation if the quotation is a complete sentence.

QUOTATIONS
"Let's go now," Sandy suggested. "Let's go now," Sandy suggested, "before it is too late."

The Word *I*

Capitalize the word *I* whenever it appears in a sentence.

EXERCISE A: Using Capitals to Begin Sentences. On the lines at the right write the words in these sentences that should be capitalized, adding the missing capitals.

EXAMPLE: we are having a party tomorrow. ___We___

1. what is the topic of your paper? _____
2. do research for your project in the library. _____
3. Oh! this is wonderful! _____
4. i am the captain of this ship. _____
5. your kidneys remove wastes from your body. _____
6. who is the star of that movie? _____
7. ouch! I hit my shoulder! _____
8. this piece of pottery was made centuries ago. _____
9. an airplane circled the field. _____
10. where is the key for the door? _____

EXERCISE B: Using Capitals in Sentences. On the lines at the right write the word or words in each sentence that should be capitalized, adding the missing capitals.

EXAMPLE: She and i are doing the science experiment together. ___I___

1. Patrick Henry said, "give me liberty or give me death!" _____
2. Carl and i are first cousins. _____
3. Mom said, "i think we made a mistake." _____
4. "this coat," Kevin explained, "belongs to my sister." _____
5. Sally, Jim, and i spent all our money at the fair. _____
6. "please listen to me," Carol said. "we must act quickly." _____
7. "this test," Jim thought, "is extremely difficult." _____
8. She and i will arrive at your house by 6:00 P.M. _____
9. "what time is it?" she asked. _____
10. "all the ingredients are here," he said. "now we can begin cooking." _____

17.2 Capitals for Proper Nouns

Names of People

Capitalize each part of a person's full name.

PEOPLE	
Barbara	R. A. Johnson
John P. Smith	Kathy O'Brien

Geographical Places

Capitalize geographical names.

GEOGRAPHICAL NAMES
Streets: Pine Avenue, Main Street *Towns and Cities:* Fairfield, London
States: Nevada, Florida *Nations:* Belgium, Burma *Continents:* Antarctica, North America
Valleys and Deserts: the Connecticut Valley, the Sahara Desert *Mountains:* the Alps, the Andes Mountains *Sections of a Country:* New England, the Northwest *Islands:* Greenland, Ireland *Scenic Spots:* The Grand Canyon, Sequoia National Park
Rivers and Falls: the Mississippi River, Niagara Falls *Lakes and Bays:* Lake Michigan, Chesapeake Bay *Seas and Oceans:* the Red Sea, the Pacific Ocean

EXERCISE A: Using Capitals for Names of People and Geographical Places. On the line at the right write the words that should be capitalized, adding the missing capitals.

EXAMPLE: We are reading poems by emily dickenson. _____Emily Dickenson_____

1. I walked home with cindy. _____

2. Is the old house on poplar street haunted? _____

3. Two of the thirteen original colonies were pennsylvania and virginia. _____

4. Bob and his family are moving to the southwest. _____

5. Have you heard of an author named c.p. snow? _____

6. I just received some new stamps from egypt for my collection. _____

7. We went to phoenix to see a professional basketball game. _____

8. Our house is only a few miles from the missouri river. _____

9. Have you ever seen the appalachian mountains? _____

10. The man who owns that store is james a. small. _____

EXERCISE B: Adding Names of People and Geographical Places to Sentences. Complete each sentence with an appropriate name of a person or geographical place.

EXAMPLE: The person leading the band is _____Roger Brown_____.

1. I just saw a film about _____ in school.

2. We went sailing on _____ last weekend.

3. The person sitting behind me in English class is _____.

4. Betty visited her aunt and uncle in _____.

5. _____ wrote that book, didn't he?

17.2 Capitals for Proper Nouns

Other Proper Nouns

Capitalize the names of specific events and periods of time. Capitalize the names of various organizations, government bodies, political parties, races, and nationalities as well as the languages spoken by different groups. Capitalize references to religions, deities, and religious scriptures. Capitalize the names of other special places and items.

SPECIFIC EVENTS AND TIMES
Historical Periods: the Middle Ages *Historical Events:* World War II *Days and Months:* Monday, August
SPECIFIC GROUPS
Organizations: the Boy Scouts *Government Bodies:* the House of Representatives *Races and Nationalities:* Chinese, American
RELIGIOUS REFERENCES
Christianity: God, the Holy Ghost, the Bible *Judaism:* the Lord, the Prophets, the Torah
OTHER SPECIAL PLACES AND ITEMS
Monuments: the Washington Monument *Buildings:* the Museum of Modern Art *Celestial Bodies:* Mars, the Big Dipper

EXERCISE A: Using Capitals for Specific Events, Times, and Groups. On the line at the right write the words in these sentences that should be capitalized, adding the missing capitals.

EXAMPLE: In 1914, world war I began. ___*World War*___

1. My father is speaking at the rotary club. _____

2. Abraham Lincoln was a member of the republican party. _____

3. labor day always occurs in september. _____

4. My brother wants to attend yale university. _____

5. Richard's mother has just started working for eastman kodak co. _____

6. Some day I hope to speak french and russian fluently. _____

7. The american revolution ended in 1783. _____

8. Each year a large group of people watches the super bowl at my house. _____

9. Yesterday we had a speaker from the defense department. _____

10. Americans held a constitutional convention in 1787. _____

EXERCISE B: Using Capitals for Religious References, Special Places, and Special Items. On the line at the right write each word that should be capitalized, adding the missing capitals.

EXAMPLE: The koran is the sacred text of Islam. ___*Koran*___

1. The talmud is a collection of ancient Jewish religious writings. _____

2. Someday I would like to visit the planet venus. _____

3. Sally Field won an oscar for her performance. _____

4. A popular brand of camera is minolta. _____

5. We saw the lincoln memorial last year. _____

17.3 Capitals for Proper Adjectives

Proper Adjectives

Capitalize most proper adjectives. Common nouns modified by proper adjectives, however, are not capitalized.

PROPER ADJECTIVES	
California oranges	*Canadian* history
Thanksgiving dinner	*Civil War* battlefield
Ivory soap	*Hollywood* stars

EXERCISE A: Using Capitals for Proper Adjectives. Underline each adjective that should be capitalized.

EXAMPLE: These <u>florida</u> summers are very hot.

1. My new dog is an english setter.
2. George received his highest grade in american history.
3. Our family is moving to the chicago suburbs.
4. Walter's grandmother baked him a german chocolate cake for his birthday.
5. I took photographs of the party with my polaroid camera.
6. Archeologists are studying the mayan temples in Mexico.
7. An old chevrolet convertible sat next to the curb.
8. This year we are planning a large christmas party.
9. My father enjoys jamaican coffee for breakfast.
10. The california condor is a rare species of bird.

EXERCISE B: Using Proper Adjectives in Sentences. Use each item below in a sentence. Capitalize the proper adjectives correctly.

EXAMPLE: (indian summer)   _This year we had a brief Indian summer in October._

1. (american flag) _____
2. (swiss cheese) _____
3. (caribbean cruise) _____
4. (crest toothpaste) _____
5. (easter vacation) _____
6. (iroquois villages) _____
7. (danish pastry) _____
8. (thanksgiving dinner) _____
9. (spanish colonies) _____
10. (buick sedan) _____

17.4 Capitals for Titles of People

Social and Professional Titles

Capitalize the title of a person when it is followed by a person's name or when it is used in direct address. Capitalize the titles of certain high government officials even when they are not followed by a person's name or used in direct address.

TITLES OF PEOPLE
Before a Noun: This class is taught by Professor Johnson.
Direct Address: Pay attention, Private Smith.
Pay attention, Private.
Titles Without a Person's Name: The President is speaking tonight.

Family Titles

Titles showing family relationships are capitalized when used with the person's name, in direct address, or when they refer to specific persons. A title after a possessive noun or pronoun is never capitalized.

FAMILY TITLES
Before a Name: We went to see *Uncle* John.
In Direct Address: "Hello, *Grandpa*," I said.
Referring to a Specific Person: Is *Grandmother* ill?
After a Possessive Noun: I met Bill's *aunt*.
After a Possessive Pronoun: His *uncle* is seventy-five.

EXERCISE A: Using Capitals for Social and Professional Titles. Underline each word that should be capitalized.

EXAMPLE: The surgeon was <u>doctor</u> Maria Carlson.

1. The king, Henry, stood on a hillside and watched the battle in the valley below.
2. Please, sir, give me your help.
3. In 1862, admiral Farragut won an important victory at New Orleans.
4. Our embassy in London was run by ambassador Kennedy.
5. The mayor has decided to seek reelection.
6. The chief justice is retiring next year.
7. Excuse me, miss, you look very familiar.
8. Have you met superintendent Ritter?
9. The sermon was delivered by reverend Peterson.
10. captain Wolfe and colonel Carlton met for dinner.

EXERCISE B: Using Capitals for Family Titles. If the family title in each sentence is correctly capitalized, put a *C* in the blank at the right. If the title is incorrectly capitalized, write the title correctly in the blank.

EXAMPLE: I visited Uncle Fred on his farm.   _*C*_

1. This year, mom became thirty-five. _____
2. Carol's aunt is head of our Girl Scout troop. _____
3. I told dad you would be late. _____
4. My sister is going steady with Mike Williams. _____
5. We saw aunt Jean on television last night. _____

17.5 Capitals for Titles of Things

Works of Art

Capitalize the first word and all other important words in the titles of books, periodicals, poems, stories, plays, paintings, and other works of art.

WORKS OF ART	
Book: *The Book of Lists*	Periodical: *Art in America*
Poem: "Mending Wall"	Story: "Of Missing Persons"

School Courses

Capitalize titles of courses when they are language courses or when they are followed by a number.

COURSES			
French	Spanish	History 201	Math 104

EXERCISE A: Using Capitals for Works of Art. Underline each word that should be capitalized in the items below.

EXAMPLE: We are reading *hamlet*.

1. I enjoy reading Robert Frost's poem "birches."
2. My parents subscribe to *american heritage*.
3. Have you ever seen Winslow Homer's painting *the gulf stream*.
4. One of O. Henry's short stories is "the gift of the magi."
5. I am starting a subscription to *civil war times*.
6. The setting for *johnny tremain* is colonial America.
7. I thought *the human comedy* was a heartwarming novel.
8. "A good man is hard to find" is one of Flannery O'Connor's most famous short stories.
9. *A farewell to arms, for whom the bell tolls*, and *the old man and the sea* are three of Ernest Hemingway's best novels.
10. Joe likes to read *fiction international*.

EXERCISE B: Using Capitals for Courses. Underline each word that should be capitalized.

EXAMPLE: I plan to take <u>french</u> next semester.

1. My favorite courses are math, chemistry, and spanish.
2. Mr. Wegmus teaches biology 101.
3. This term my sister is taking algebra II.
4. My brother is planning to take greek in college.
5. Chico is taking introduction to modern american fiction as his elective course.

17.6 Capitals in Letters

Using Capitals in Letters

Capitalize the first word and all nouns in letter salutations and the first word in letter closings.

LETTERS
Salutations: Dear Mrs. Smith, Dear Uncle Joe, *Closings:* Sincerely yours, Love,

EXERCISE A: Using Capitals for Letter Salutations and Closings. Rewrite each of these letter parts, adding the missing capitals.

EXAMPLE: sincerely,   _Sincerely,_

1. dear aunt edith, _____
2. dear sister, _____
3. very truly yours, _____
4. yours sincerely, _____
5. dear sarah, _____
6. with warmest regards, _____
7. your friend, _____
8. affectionately, _____
9. dear dr. hopkins, _____
10. dear jack, _____

EXERCISE B: Using Capitals in Letters. Write a short letter of one paragraph inviting a friend to visit you. Use capital letters where they are needed throughout your letter.

_____
_____
_____

_____ ,
_____
_____
_____
_____
_____

_____ ,
_____

18.1 Abbreviations of Titles of People

Social Titles

Abbreviations of social titles before a proper name begin with a capital letter and end with a period.

ABBREVIATIONS OF SOCIAL TITLES
Mr. Romero
Mrs. Harris
Messrs. Jeffers and Rogers

Other Titles

Abbreviations of other titles used before proper names also begin with a capital letter and end with a period. In most formal writing these titles should be spelled out.

ABBREVIATIONS OF TITLES BEFORE NAMES			
Gov.	Governor	Maj.	Major
Pres.	President	Dr.	Doctor
Capt.	Captain	Fr.	Father

Abbreviations of titles after a name start with a capital and end with a period. They can be used in any type of writing.

ABBREVIATIONS OF TITLES AFTER NAMES			
Jr.	Junior	M.D.	Doctor of Medicine
Sr.	Senior	R.N.	Registered Nurse

EXERCISE A: Using Abbreviations for Titles of People. In the space at the right, write the proper abbreviation for each title in these sentences.

EXAMPLE: Mister Harris missed the bus. _Mr._

1. Roger Hartley, senior, is my father. _____
2. Doctor O'Brien has a large examining room. _____
3. Next week I have an appointment with Janet Macaluso, Doctor of Dental Surgery. _____
4. Madame Pompidou is our new French teacher. _____
5. Professor Herbert Friedman is my brother's freshman advisor. _____
6. Harold Vaughn, Junior, has just started running his father's business. _____
7. Margaret Wilde, Registered Nurse, was on duty that evening. _____
8. The ancient history course was taught by Vincent Miano, Doctor of Philosophy. _____
9. Our football coach this season is Mister Frank Putnam. _____
10. The kidney surgery was performed by Doctor Adair. _____

EXERCISE B: More Work with Abbreviations. Write the correct abbreviation next to each item.

EXAMPLE: Senator _Sen._

1. Governor _____
2. Ensign _____
3. Reverend _____
4. President _____
5. Major _____
6. Honorable _____
7. Brother _____
8. Ambassador _____
9. Professor _____
10. Treasurer _____

18.2 Abbreviations for Time and Historical Dates

Time

For abbreviations of time before noon and after noon, either capital letters followed by periods or small letters followed by periods are acceptable. These abbreviations can be used in any type of writing, but only with numerals.

ABBREVIATIONS FOR TIME
Abbreviations: A.M. or a.m. (*ante meridian,* before noon)
P.M. or p.m. (*post meridian,* after noon)
With Numerals: A lunar eclipse will occur at 3:00 P.M.
Without Numerals: I will meet him at five o'clock this afternoon.

Dates

Abbreviations for historical dates before and after the birth of Christ require capital letters followed by periods. They can be used in any type of writing.

ABBREVIATIONS FOR DATES
Abbreviations: B.C. (before Christ)
A.D. (*anno Domini,* in the year of the Lord)
Examples: Caesar died in 44 B.C.
The Pilgrims landed in America in 1620 A.D. (or A.D. 1620)

EXERCISE A: Using Abbreviations for Time. In these sentences, write the correct abbreviation for the unit of time in the space at the right. If the unit of time should remain as it is, write a *C* in the space.

EXAMPLE: I arose at 6:30 *in the morning* to go birdwatching. ___A.M. or a.m.___

1. The matinee performance begins at 2:30 *in the afternoon.* _____
2. The film about Napoleon will be shown in the cafeteria at 10:15 *in the morning.* _____
3. This train leaves at precisely four o'clock *in the afternoon.* _____
4. The kickoff is scheduled for 1:00 *in the afternoon.* _____
5. My favorite television show has been delayed until ten o'clock *this evening.* _____
6. According to the schedule, another bus leaves at 3:17 *in the afternoon.* _____
7. Our meeting has been rescheduled until Friday at 9:30 *in the morning.* _____
8. The plane leaves at 11:15 *in the morning,* and I don't want to be late.
9. I am supposed to meet her for dinner at seven o'clock *this evening.* _____
10. The clock in the bedroom reads 7:00 *in the morning.* _____

EXERCISE B: Using Abbreviations for Dates. Write the correct abbreviation for each date in parentheses.

EXAMPLE: The Battle of Marathon was fought in (490 before Christ). ___490 B.C.___

1. In (201 before Christ) Hannibal was defeated at Zama. _____
2. Charlemagne was crowned Holy Roman Emperor in (800 in the year of the lord). _____
3. Cicero was born in (106 before Christ). _____
4. The Normans conquered England at the Battle of Hastings in (1066 in the year of the Lord). _____
5. In (1776 in the year of the Lord) the Declaration of Independence was signed. _____

18.3 Geographical Abbreviations

Using Geographical Abbreviations

Abbreviations for geographical terms before or after a proper noun begin with a capital letter and end with a period. They are seldom used in formal writing.

ABBREVIATIONS OF GEOGRAPHICAL TERMS			
Ave.	Avenue	Mt.	Mountain
Co.	County	Rd.	Road
Is.	Island	St.	Street

Traditional abbreviations for states begin with a capital letter and end with a period. The official Postal Service abbreviations for states require capital letters with no periods. Abbreviations for states are generally not used in formal writing.

ABBREVIATIONS FOR STATES		
State	**Traditional**	**Postal Service**
Arkansas	Ark.	AR
Florida	Fla.	FL
Maine	Me.	ME
New Jersey	N.J.	NJ
Vermont	Vt.	VT

EXERCISE A: Using Abbreviations for Geographical Terms. Write the abbreviation for each of the underlined geographical terms.

EXAMPLE: 53 Harley <u>Avenue</u>   *Ave.*

1. Empire State <u>Building</u> _____
2. Cape Breton <u>Island</u> _____
3. Baldwin <u>County</u>, Georgia _____
4. <u>Mount</u> Washington _____
5. Grand Teton National <u>Park</u> _____

6. 34 Willow <u>Street</u> _____
7. <u>Route</u> 6 _____
8. 807 Seminole <u>Boulevard</u> _____
9. <u>Province</u> of Manitoba _____
10. Pulaski <u>Highway</u> _____

EXERCISE B: Using Abbreviations for States. For each state, write the type of abbreviation described in the parentheses.

EXAMPLE: Montgomery, Alabama (traditional)   *Ala.*

1. Phoenix, *Arizona* (Postal Service) _____
2. Litchfield Co., *Connecticut* (traditional) _____
3. St. Louis, *Missouri* (traditional) _____
4. 390 Main Street, Cleveland, *Ohio* (Postal Service) _____
5. Kiowa Co., *Colorado* (Postal Service) _____
6. Boise, *Idaho* (traditional) _____
7. Tampa, *Florida* (Postal Service) _____
8. 2120 College Street, Cedar Falls, *Iowa* (Postal Service) _____
9. 215 Congress Street, Boston, *Massachusetts* (traditional) _____
10. Roswell County, *New Mexico* (traditional) _____

18.4 Abbreviations of Measurements

Traditional Measurements

With traditional measurements use small letters and periods to form the abbreviations. These abbreviations are not used in formal writing except with numerals.

TRADITIONAL MEASUREMENTS					
in.	inch(es)	tsp.	teaspoon(s)	pt.	pint(s)
ft.	foot; feet	tbsp.	tablespoon(s)	qt.	quart(s)
yd.	yard(s)	oz.	ounce(s)	gal.	gallon(s)
mi.	mile(s)	lb.	pound(s)	F.	Fahrenheit

Metric Measurements

With metric measurements use small letters and no periods to form the abbreviations. These abbreviations are not used in formal writing except with numerals.

METRIC MEASUREMENTS					
g	gram(s)	mm	millimeter(s)	L	liter(s)
kg	kilogram(s)	cm	centimeter(s)	C	Celsius
		m	meter(s)		
		km	kilometer(s)		

EXERCISE A: Using Abbreviations for Traditional Measurements. Write out the word or words that each abbreviation stands for.

EXAMPLE: gal. _gallon(s)_

1. yd. _____
2. mi. _____
3. ft. _____
4. F. _____
5. qt. _____

6. oz. _____
7. pt. _____
8. tsp. _____
9. tbsp. _____
10. lb. _____

EXERCISE B: Using Abbreviations for Metric Measurements. Write the abbreviation for each metric measurement.

EXAMPLE: gram(s) _g_

1. kilometer(s) ____
2. liter(s) ____
3. Celsius ____

4. kilogram ____
5. millimeter ____

19.1 End Marks

Uses of the Period

Use a period to end a declarative sentence, an imperative sentence, and an indirect question. Use a period to end most abbreviations.

PERIODS
Declarative Sentence: Theodore Roosevelt was President of the United States.
Imperative Sentence: Drive straight ahead.
Indirect Question: I asked where we were going.
Abbreviations: Mr. Rd. Tenn. Mt.

Uses of the Question Mark

Use a question mark to end an interrogative sentence. Use a question mark to end an incomplete question in which the rest of the question is understood. Use a question mark to end a statement that is intended as a question.

QUESTION MARKS
Interrogative Sentence: Who are you?
Incomplete Question: Certainly, we should have lunch. Where?
Statement Intended as a Question: We are early?

Uses of the Exclamation Mark

Use an exclamation mark to end an exclamatory sentence or an imperative sentence if the command is urgent and forceful. Use an exclamation mark after an interjection expressing strong emotion.

EXCLAMATION MARKS
Exclamatory Sentence: That was a wonderful trip!
Imperative Sentence: Be quiet!
Interjection: Wow! This is fun.

EXERCISE A: Using End Marks Correctly. Add the proper end mark to each item.

EXAMPLE: What a great name for a dog ___!___

1. The Egyptians wrote on papyrus ___.___
2. Which way is the stadium ___?___
3. Ouch ___.___ That hurts.
4. Tell me your name ___.___
5. Where did you find this ___?___

6. We asked why she left ___.___
7. L ___.___ Butterfield
8. Look out ___.___
9. Austria is in central Europe ___.___
10. Who is the Prime Minister ___?___

idk

EXERCISE B: Supplying Ending Marks. Write the kinds of sentences listed below. Be sure to use correct end marks.

EXAMPLE: Question ___*Which briefcase is mine?*___

1. Question ___Where are we going?___
2. Indirect Question ___I asked where we were going.___
3. Declarative Sentence ___George Washington was president of U.S.___
4. Exclamatory Sentence ___That was an awesome adventure!___
5. Imperative Sentence ___Pay attention!___

19.2 Commas That Separate Basic Elements

Commas with Compound Sentences

Use a comma before the conjunction to separate two independent clauses in a compound sentence.

COMPOUND SENTENCES
I cooked dinner, and Glenda set the table.
We waited for John, but he never arrived.

Commas Between Items in a Series

Use commas to separate three or more words, phrases, or clauses in a series.

SERIES
Firs, spruces, and pines are evergreen trees.
They traveled out of New York, through Pennsylvania, and into Ohio.

Commas Between Adjectives

Use commas to separate adjectives of equal rank. Do not use commas to separate adjectives that must stay in a specific order.

ADJECTIVES
With Commas: He drove a shiny, green sedan.
Without Commas: The attic was filled with many old clothes.

EXERCISE A: Using Commas Correctly. Add commas where they are required.

EXAMPLE: Bill left the party and he went home.
              Bill left the party, and he went home.

1. Native Americans grew corn, beans, and tomatoes.
2. The sleek, powerful leopard, raced toward its prey.
3. The road ran around the mountain across the river, and into the town.
4. We approached the medieval castle with its old drawbridge huge towers, and broad moat.
5. Following the directions, thinking carefully, and taking your time will insure success on the project.
6. The California condor, the Wyoming toad, and the red fox are endangered species.
7. Charles did his best, but he still lost the race.
8. Claire saw two of her friends in the grandstand, so she went to sit with them.
9. That large, heavy bag, is mine.
10. California, Oregon, and Washington border the Pacific Ocean.

EXERCISE B: Understanding the Uses of Commas. These sentences are punctuated correctly. Identify the use of commas by writing the words *compound sentence, series,* or *adjectives.*

EXAMPLE: Ed wrote letters, and then he listened to music.   *compound sentence*

1. Alberta, Ontario, and Quebec are Canadian provinces. _Series_
2. The quick, brown fox outran the shaggy dog. _adjective_
3. With hard work, with the right skills, and with a little luck you can be successful. _____
4. Dad and I left for the airport at noon, yet we were still late for Mom's plane. _____
5. Several noisy squirrels lived in the oak tree. _____

19.3 Commas That Set Off Added Elements

Commas After Introductory Material

Use a comma after an introductory word, phrase, or clause.

INTRODUCTORY MATERIAL
Introductory Word: Yes, Jim is our best debater. *Introductory Phrase:* With very little money, she left home for the big city. *Introductory Adverb Clause:* After he finished school, Dick joined the Army.

Commas with Parenthetical Expressions

Use commas to set off parenthetical expressions.

PARENTHETICAL EXPRESSIONS
Names of People Being Addressed: That's the right answer, Doug. *Certain Adverbs:* We chose, therefore, not to go. *Common Expressions:* This solution, I think, is the best. *Contrasting Expressions:* The river is long, not deep.

EXERCISE A: Using Commas After Introductory Material. Write the introductory word, phrase, or clause in each sentence, and add the needed comma.

EXAMPLE: Remember you have only thirty minutes for this section of the test.   *Remember,*

1. After the brief rain shower had ended the sun began to shine. _____

2. No this is the wrong answer. _____

3. With all the energy he could muster the old man tried to speak. _____

4. To win the district championship we practiced day and night. _____

5. Please isn't there someone who can help me? _____

6. With only a compass and a canteen of water he set out across the desert.
_____

7. Sarah stop talking and listen to me. _____

8. To escape capture by the police the fugitive hid in an abandoned cave.
_____

9. Certainly we should begin to plan the school fair as soon as possible.
_____

10. After I saw that movie I could understand why it won an Oscar. _____

EXERCISE B: Using Commas with Parenthetical Expressions. Use the following parenthetical expressions in sentences. Correctly punctuate these expressions with commas.

EXAMPLE: however   *This dog, however, is not ours.*

1. nevertheless _____

2. I believe _____

3. of course _____

4. therefore _____

5. not yours _____

19.3 Commas That Set Off Added Elements

Commas with Nonessential Expressions

Use commas to set off nonessential expressions. These expressions are additional phrases or clauses that can be left out. Expressions that are essential cannot be left out without changing the meaning of the sentence.

ESSENTIAL AND NONESSENTIAL EXPRESSIONS

Essential: The Hollywood star *Clark Gable* appeared in this film.

Nonessential: Clark Gable, *the Hollywood star,* appeared in this film.

Essential: The old man *smiling broadly* is my grandfather.

Nonessential: The old man, *smiling broadly,* took the little boy in his arms.

Essential: I am looking for a beautiful gift *which is inexpensive.*

Nonessential: I bought this beautiful gift, *which is inexpensive,* at the local hardware store.

EXERCISE A: Using Commas with Nonessential Expressions. Add commas to set off nonessential expressions. Not every sentence contains a nonessential expression.

EXAMPLE: That house which was built in 1802 belonged to the first mayor of our town.
That house, which was built in 1802, belonged to the first mayor of our town.

1. Ernest Hemingway the famous author wrote *The Old Man and the Sea*.
2. The two soldiers hastening to join their battalion were unaware that the enemy followed them.
3. The table which you gave your brother must have been difficult to build.
4. Captain Wilson standing on the deck of his ship looked out toward the horizon.
5. My sister staring absentmindedly out the window didn't hear me speak to her.
6. The harvest moon which shone brightly that evening illuminated the entire countryside.
7. Jimmy Carter the former President was also governor of Georgia.
8. We are only hiring people who have computer skills.
9. Karl who is graduating this year has been a tremendous asset to the school.
10. The play which we are planning to see has received very favorable reviews.

EXERCISE B: Writing Essential and Nonessential Expressions. Complete each sentence with an appropriate expression. Set off the nonessential expressions with commas.

EXAMPLE: The dog, ___*a Labrador retriever,*___ was very friendly.

1. The British soldiers _____ began to fire on the enemy.
2. This coat _____ is extremely warm.
3. Willa Cather _____ wrote *My Antonia*.
4. The Romans _____ were great builders.
5. The song _____ is very popular in England.
6. The binoculars _____ are excellent for birdwatching.
7. This year we are taking our vacation at Nature Lake _____.
8. That cat _____ belongs to my brother.
9. The man _____ is our history teacher.
10. This is a painting of Paul Revere _____

19.3 Commas That Set Off Added Elements

Commas with Dates and Geographical Names

When a date is made up of two or more parts, use a comma after each item except when a month is followed by a day. When a geographical name is made up of two or more parts, use a comma after each item.

DATES AND GEOGRAPHICAL NAMES
Date: Thursday, March 14, is my birthday.
Geographical Name: My family is moving to Cleveland, Ohio, tomorrow.

Other Uses of the Comma

Use commas in the situations shown in the chart below.

OTHER USES OF THE COMMA
Address: Send the letter to Roger Brown, 1160 Battery Street, San Francisco, California 94120.
Salutation and Closing: Dear Bob, Sincerely,
Numbers: 69,486 miles
Direct Quotations: "I'll see you tonight," Gail said, "after the play is over."
To Prevent Confusion: After studying, Peter went outside to play ball.

EXERCISE A: Using Commas with Dates and Geographical Names. Insert commas where they are needed.

EXAMPLE: On October 5, 1685 our town was founded.
         On October 5, 1685, our town was founded.

1. The Battle of Gettysburg began on July 1 1863.
2. Montgomery Alabama was the first capital of the Confederacy.
3. My grandparents moved from Hartford Connecticut to Tampa Florida.
4. In April 1985 our community held its bicentennial.
5. The English nobles forced King John to sign the Magna Carta in June 1215.
6. My parents celebrated their fifteenth wedding anniversary on August 18 1984.
7. John's ancestors come from Warsaw Poland.
8. Before August 1959 America had only forty-nine states.
9. On October 19 1781 the British surrendered at Yorktown.
10. We have moved here from Salem Oregon.

EXERCISE B: Using Commas in Other Situations. Add commas where they are needed.

EXAMPLE: There were 50289 people in the stadium.
         There were 50,289 people in the stadium.

1. Mail this letter to Brian Johnson 110 Merton Street Fairfield Connecticut 06430.
2. Sincerely
   Bill
3. Outside Bob breathed a sigh of relief.
4. "These are the times that try men's souls" wrote Thomas Paine.
5. The state of New Mexico has an area of 122666 square miles.
6. Dear Susan
7. "Let's go to the park" Laura suggested "and have a picnic."
8. Their office is located at 150 Main Street Wilbraham Massachusetts.
9. The general had 45000 men in his army.
10. My new address is 2840 Haskell Avenue Dallas Texas 75221.

19.4 The Semicolon

Semicolons Used to Join Independent Clauses

Use a semicolon to join independent clauses that are not already joined by the conjunctions *and, or, nor, for, but, so,* or *yet.* Semicolons may also be used to join independent clauses separated by either a conjunctive adverb or a transitional expression.

SEMICOLONS AND INDEPENDENT CLAUSES

No Conjunction: Sarah's best subject is math; John's is science.
Conjunctive Adverb: We expect to win easily; nevertheless we are still practicing very hard.
Transitional Expression: His sister is an outstanding poet; as a result, she won the school poetry contest.

Semicolons Used to Avoid Confusion

A semicolon may be used to avoid confusion when independent clauses or items in a series already contain commas.

SEMICOLON TO AVOID CONFUSION

This school, which is located at the east end of town, was built only a few years ago; but it will have to be closed now because enrollment is so low.

EXERCISE A: Using Semicolons Correctly. In each sentence a comma is used instead of a semicolon. Circle the comma to show that a semicolon is needed.

EXAMPLE: Ken slept late,⊙as a result, he missed his bus.

1. George decided not to walk to work, it was too far, and he had too little time.
2. Running through the park, Gail tripped, she scraped her knee badly.
3. I thought Barry's painting was excellent, in fact, it was the best in the show.
4. Pack a warm sweater for the trip, otherwise, you will be cold at night.
5. The tulips, which looked so beautiful this spring, were planted only last fall, however, we will have to move them when we build the new garage.
6. During the Golden Age of Greece, playwrights wrote great tragedies, they also wrote brilliant comedies.
7. If we expect to have this paper finished by May 15, we can't waste any time, therefore, let's begin planning it today.
8. After the plane had landed, mechanics checked its engines, as a result, they decided to ground the aircraft for three days.
9. If I am not awake by five o'clock, call me, otherwise, I will be late for work.
10. The man did not show up for his appointment that morning, instead, he left town.

EXERCISE B: Writing Compound Sentences with Semicolons. Complete these sentences.

EXAMPLE: _I like to fish_ ; however, _I do not enjoy baiting the hook_ .

1. _____; however,_____.
2. _____; instead, _____.
3. _____; for instance, _____.
4. _____; in fact, _____.
5. _____; moreover, _____.

19.5 The Colon

The Colon as an Introductory Device

Use a colon before a list of items following an independent clause.

COLON BEFORE A LIST
We traveled to three cities: Chicago, St. Louis, and Kansas City.

Special Uses of the Colon

Use a colon in a number of special writing situations.

SPECIAL USES OF THE COLON	
Numerals Giving the Time	4:30 P.M. 8:00 A.M.
Salutations in Business Letters	Dear Sir:
Labels Used to Signal	Warning: Keep this medication out
Important Ideas	of the reach of children.

EXERCISE A: Using Colons as Introductory Devices. Add colons where they are needed. Not every sentence needs a colon.

EXAMPLE: We bought three items a pencil, a pen, and an eraser.
We bought three items: a pencil, a pen, and an eraser.

1. This semester we are studying several civilizations Egyptian, Greek, and Roman.
2. My list for camp includes the following items of clothing shirts, shorts, sneakers, socks, sweaters, and swimming suits.
3. We saw many types of dogs at the show collies, setters, poodles, beagles, and boxers.
4. Dad and I planted three trees a pine, a birch, and a red maple.
5. Barbara's favorite colors were blue, yellow, and pink.

EXERCISE B: Using Colons in Special Situations. Add colons where necessary in the items below.

EXAMPLE: 600 A.M.
6:00 A.M.

1. Dear Mr. Harper
2. Notice This building is closed until September 15.
3. Caution Wash hands after use.
4. Dear Taxpayer
5. 1140 P.M.
6. Gentlemen
7. Warning Substance is harmful if swallowed.
8. 1219 A.M.
9. Dosage Two tablets three or four times daily.
10. Dear Madam/Sir

19.6 Quotation Marks with Direct Quotations

Direct and Indirect Quotations

A direct quotation represents a person's exact speech or thoughts and is enclosed in quotation marks (" "). An indirect quotation reports the general meaning of what a person said or thought and does not require quotation marks.

DIRECT AND INDIRECT QUOTATIONS	
Direct Quotations:	"Set the table for breakfast," Dad said.
	"Are you ready?" she asked.
Indirect Quotations:	Bill said that he would help me.
	Carol asked why we were going.

Direct Quotations with Introductory, Concluding, and Interrupting Expressions

Expressions such as *he asked* are often used to identify the speaker in a direct quotation. These expressions can begin, conclude, or interrupt a quotation.

PUNCTUATING DIRECT QUOTATIONS	
Introductory Expression	Barbara said, "Let's shovel the snow."
Concluding Expression	"I am happy," said Bill.
	"Will you join us tomorrow?" we asked.
	"Hurry!" everyone yelled.
Interrupting Expression	"That," we were informed, "is a snow leopard."
Two Sentences	"This is not the right way," George said. "I think we made a wrong turn at the last corner."

EXERCISE A: Punctuating Direct Quotations. Place quotation marks, commas, and other punctuation marks where they are required.

EXAMPLE: Mark said I understand what you want me to do.
Mark said, "I understand what you want me to do."

1. The parakeet in that cage Walter explained is named Polly.
2. I wonder if you sell tape Pam asked.
3. We asked when Halley's comet would appear.
4. This book he said was written by Barbara Tuchman.
5. Pass me the ball Sam yelled. I can score a touchdown.
6. Let's go they shouted.
7. The dentist said you have no cavities.
8. This play Claire announced has been canceled.
9. Will you show me your pottery I asked the clerk. I would like to buy a gift for someone.
10. These Native American villages the guide explained were abandoned centuries ago.

EXERCISE B: Writing Direct Quotations. Complete these sentences.

EXAMPLE: I asked, _"When was this museum opened?"_

1. Carol said, "_____."

2. "_____," he explained, "_____."

3. "_____?" we asked.

4. "_____!" they exclaimed.

5. "_____," he announced.

19.6 Quotation Marks with Direct Quotations

Quotation Marks with Other Punctuation Marks

Place a comma or a period inside the final quotation mark. Place a question mark or exclamation mark inside the final quotation mark if the end mark is part of the quotation and outside if the end mark is part of the entire sentence, not the quotation.

QUOTATION MARKS AND OTHER PUNCTUATION MARKS	
Commas and Periods:	"This car has a flat tire," Dad said.
Question Marks and Exclamation Marks Inside Final Quotation Marks:	Karl asked, "What is the homework assignment for today?"
Question Marks and Exclamation Marks Outside Final Quotation Marks:	I'm surprised that you can say, "I'm guilty"!

Quotation Marks for Dialogue

When writing dialogue, begin a new paragraph with each change of speaker.

DIALOGUE
"Where are you traveling?" the old man asked me. He was looking at me with great curiosity.   "I'm visiting my aunt and uncle in Los Angeles," I announced.

EXERCISE A: Punctuating Direct Quotations. One or two punctuation marks have been left out of each sentence. Add them correctly to the sentences.

EXAMPLE: Ken asked, "What am I supposed to do"
            Ken asked, "What am I supposed to do?"

1. The umpire shouted, "Play ball"
2. "There will be a full moon tonight" he said.
3. "How are we going to explain this to Mom" Connie asked.
4. Bill announced "The library is closing in fifteen minutes"
5. Has anyone said, "You are lying"
6. He screamed, "Stop the car"
7. "Wait a minute" I shouted.
8. "I need a new pair of sneakers for track" Clara said
9. Bob asked "When does the planetarium show begin"
10. "Do these math problems ever become any easier" I wondered.

EXERCISE B: Paragraphing Dialogue. Circle the first word in each sentence that requires indentation for a new paragraph.

"This library is enormous," Jim said. "Where should we begin?" "I think the best place to start is the card catalog," Kathy suggested. "Yes," Jim agreed, "we can just look under our subject, *Sioux Indians*." "We'll find all the books in the library that might help us," Kathy said. "Then we can look in the periodical section," Jim added. Kathy smiled. "That will give us plenty of information for our paper."

19.7 Underlining and Other Uses of Quotation Marks

When to Underline

Underline the titles of long written works, publications published as a single work, movies, television and radio series, and works of music and art. Underline the names of individual air, sea, space, and land craft.

WORKS THAT ARE UNDERLINED
Title of a Book: The Deerslayer
Title of a Play: King Lear
Title of a Movie: Star Wars
Title of a Television Series: Benson
Title of a Painting: Night Watch
Name of Sea Craft: the Lusitania
Number Used as Name: Thirteen is an unlucky number.

When to Use Quotation Marks

Use quotation marks around the titles of short written works, episodes in a series, songs, parts of a long musical composition, and the title of a work that is mentioned as part of a collection.

WORKS WITH QUOTATION MARKS
Title of a Short Story: "The Purloined Letter"
Title of an Article: "How to Train Your Dog"
Title of a Song: "Night and Day"

EXERCISE A: Punctuating Different Types of Works. Use underlining or quotation marks with the works in each sentence.

EXAMPLE: I went to see the play Cats.
    I went to see the play Cats.

1. Carol read that article in Newsweek.
2. Dad enjoys Cole Porter's song I Get a Kick Out of You.
3. We heard Appalachian Spring performed by the local symphony orchestra.
4. The President quoted The Wall Street Journal in his speech.
5. Mom's article, Balancing Your Career and Your Family, will be published next month.
6. The movie Amadeus deserved to win so many Oscar awards.
7. My uncle has a leading role in the play Kiss Me, Kate.
8. In his book, The American Family, I enjoyed chapter six, The Single-Parent Family.
9. Sesame Street is extremely popular with children.
10. Fifteen has always been my lucky number.

EXERCISE B: Choosing the Correct Form. Circle the correct form below.

EXAMPLE: The magazine "Time" or (Time)

1. Chekov's play The Seagull or "The Seagull"
2. An article titled My Life or "My Life"
3. Longfellow's long poem The Song of Hiawatha or "The Song of Hiawatha"
4. The Apollo 8 spacecraft or the "Apollo 8" spacecraft
5. A chapter entitled "The Ageless Ones" or The Ageless Ones

19.8 The Hyphen

When to Use the Hyphen

A hyphen is used to form numbers from twenty-one to ninety-nine and with fractions that are used as adjectives. Hyphens are also used with certain prefixes and suffixes, and with certain compound nouns and modifiers. Do not use hyphens with compound proper adjectives or modifiers that include a word ending in *ly*.

USES OF THE HYPHEN
With Numbers: seventy-five books
With Fractions Used as Adjectives: the three-fifths rule
Prefixes and Suffixes: post-season game ex-senator
Compound Nouns: great-grandmother
Compound Modifiers: once-a-month meeting

Rules for Dividing Words at the End of a Line

Divide words only between syllables. Do not divide a word so that a single letter stands alone and do not divide proper nouns or proper adjectives. Divide a hyphenated word only after the hyphen.

DIVIDING WORDS	
Correct	**Incorrect**
mid-dle	midd-le
afar	a-far
Henry	Hen-ry
great-granddaughter	great-grand-daughter

EXERCISE A: Using Hyphens. Put hyphens where they are necessary.

EXAMPLE: We have thirty three volunteers.
        We have thirty-three volunteers.

1. Our team won the pre season contest.
2. The president elect spoke to our school.
3. A long awaited opportunity had finally presented itself.
4. We visited my great grandfather over the holiday.
5. A terrible mid air collision occurred on Saturday.
6. The candidate's pro union sympathies were very obvious.
7. His success in school helped build Roger's self confidence.
8. Calvin was a mean spirited man.
9. The ex governor has decided to run for the Senate.
10. I watched the slow motion pictures of the game.

EXERCISE B: Hyphenating Words. Draw vertical lines between syllables that can be divided at the end of a line. Do nothing to words that cannot be divided.

EXAMPLES: butter   but/ter
        lane

1. adopt	3. rooted	5. harbor	7. glass	9. among
2. helpful	4. carpet	6. bookstore	8. football	10. birthday

19.9 The Apostrophe

Apostrophes with Possessive Nouns

Form the possessive of nouns according to the following rules.

FORMING POSSESSIVE NOUNS	
Add an apostrophe and an -s to show the possessive of most singular nouns.	father's car Dave's book boss's office
Add just an apostrophe to show the possessive case of plural nouns ending in -s or -es.	dogs' owner churches' congregations
Add an apostrophe and -s to show the possessive case of plural nouns that do not end in -s or -es.	the four men's cars the geese's honking
Add an apostrophe and -s (or just an apostrophe if the word is a plural ending in -s) to the last word of a compound noun to form the possessive.	high school's mascot Boy Scouts' trip president-elect's speech

Apostrophes with Pronouns

Use an apostrophe and -s with indefinite pronouns to show possession. Do not use an apostrophe with possessive personal pronouns.

POSSESSIVE FORMS OF PRONOUNS		
Indefinite		**Personal**
another's	one another's	my, mine, our,
anybody's	somebody's	ours, your, yours,
each other's	no one's	his, her, hers, its, their, theirs

EXERCISE A: Writing Possessive Forms. In the space at the right write the possessive form of each item.

EXAMPLE: The money of his father _____*his father's money*_____

1. the toys of the children _____
2. the tents of the circus _____
3. the barn of the horses _____
4. the business of no one _____
5. the house of our sister-in-law _____

EXERCISE B: Using Possessives. Complete each sentence with a possessive noun or pronoun.

EXAMPLE: _____*Ken's*_____ paper is excellent.

1. _____ footprints were in the snow.
2. _____ book was a bestseller.
3. _____ party was the most successful year.
4. He owns a store that sells _____ clothes.
5. The _____ secretary is on vacation this week.

19.9 The Apostrophe

Apostrophes with Contractions

Use an apostrophe in a contraction to show the position of the missing letter or letters. The most common contractions are formed with verbs.

COMMON CONTRACTIONS WITH VERBS		
Verb + *not*	aren't (are not) didn't (did not)	isn't (is not) can't (cannot)
Pronoun + the verb *will*	I'll (I will)	they'll (they will)
Pronoun or noun + the verb *be*	it's (it is)	Bob's (Bob is)
Pronoun or noun + the verb *would*	she'd (she would) Betsy'd (Betsy would)	

Special Uses of the Apostrophe

Use an apostrophe and -s to write the plurals of numbers, symbols, letters, and words used to name themselves.

SPECIAL USES OF THE APOSTROPHE
three *6*'s   four *?*'s Roll your *r*'s. Always capitalize *I*'s in sentences.

EXERCISE A: Using Contractions Correctly. Each sentence contains a word group that can be written as a contraction. Write each contraction in the space at the right.

EXAMPLE: We are not leaving now.   ___*aren't*___

1. Carol is singing in the choir. _____
2. Who is your homeroom teacher? _____
3. You should not leave your roller skates in the driveway. _____
4. Where is my cookbook? _____
5. I would not do that if I were you. _____
6. He would do that for you. _____
7. They were not expected home until 6:00 P.M. _____
8. You will be late for school. _____
9. Who will help me with this problem? _____
10. Roger is selling his crafts at the fair. _____

EXERCISE B: Using Contractions in Sentences. Fill in each blank with an appropriate contraction.

EXAMPLE: ___*She's*___   at college this year.

1. _____ the cap for the bottle of mayonnaise?
2. My phone number has two _____ in it.
3. There are three _____ in banana.
4. She _____ my choice for class president.
5. _____ see me in the morning.

20.1 Prewriting

Exploring Ideas

To explore ideas for writing topics, think about your interests, experiences, and ideas.

TECHNIQUES FOR GENERATING IDEAS	
Interviewing Yourself	Ask yourself questions to discover topics that interest you.
Free Writing	Write anything that comes into your mind.
Journal Writing	Keep a daily record of your thoughts, feelings, and experiences.
Reading and Saving	Read as much and as often as possible.
Clustering	Think of words associated with a chosen topic.
Brainstorming	Start with an idea and build on it, trying to go in as many directions as possible.
Cueing	Use a variety of devices to stimulate ideas.

Choosing and Narrowing a Topic

Choose a topic that you can effectively cover in the allotted amount of space.

EXERCISE A: Interviewing Yourself. Answer the questions below to help you generate ideas for potential writing topics.

1. What activities do you enjoy? _____

_____

2. In what areas do you have special skills or knowledge? _____

_____

3. What kinds of subjects are you interested in? _____

_____

4. To whom do you like to speak and about what topics? _____

_____

5. What has happened to you in the past or is happening to you now that seems of special interest?

_____

EXERCISE B: Free Writing. On separate paper, write for ten minutes, nonstop, on any of the following topics. Don't worry about spelling or punctuation. Just keep writing. Start with general reactions and move on to specific ones. Include any sights, sounds, or other details associated with the subject.

Summer vacation	Living in the city
Walking through the woods	Losing a close friend
Cold weather	Baseball
Winning an important game	Walking beside the ocean
Striving to reach a goal	An unpleasant situation
Waking up early in the morning	Going to school

20.1 Prewriting

Determining an Audience and Purpose

Determine your audience and purpose before you begin writing.

Developing a Main Idea and Support

State a main idea. Then gather and organize supporting information to develop it effectively.

ORGANIZATION OF SUPPORTING INFORMATION	
Chronological Order	Information arranged in the order in which it happened in time
Order of Importance	Information arranged from least to most important, or vice versa
Comparison and Contrast	Information arranged according to similarities and differences between items
Developmental	Information arranged so that one point leads logically to the next

EXERCISE A: Determining Audience and Purpose. Choose one of the five broad topics below. Then complete the work that follows.

Music   Politics   Space travel   History   Sports

1. Use the clustering technique to narrow the topic you have chosen to one that is narrow enough to be covered in a short paper. Then write your topic. _____

_____

2. Write a possible purpose for your paper. _____

3. Write another possible purpose for your paper. _____

4. Identify a potential audience for the purpose you wrote in #2. _____

_____

5. Identify a potential audience for the purpose you wrote in #3. _____

_____

EXERCISE B: Developing a Topic. Complete the work below to develop your topic from Exercise A.

1. Decide on your main idea. _____

_____

2. Make a list of supporting information. _____

_____

_____

_____

_____

3. Choose a method for organizing the information you wrote in #2. _____

_____

4. Arrange your information according to the method you chose in #3. _____

_____

_____

_____

20.2 Writing

Writing a First Draft

Translate your prewriting notes into sentences and paragraphs, without worrying about punctuation, spelling, grammar, or fine tuning.

SAMPLE ROUGH DRAFT

The foreign student exchange program is very important. There are many reasons why it is important. Throughout the world, young boys and girls represent the future leaders of their countries. Because of this, it is important for boys and girls to learn to understand people from other countries and cultures at an early age. The student exchange program allows students to live with families in foreign countries for extended periods of time and to discover firsthand what it is like to be a part of another culture. Students can learn about the special needs and concerns of the people in the country they are visiting. Hopefully, in the end they will learn that while people from other countries are different in many ways, they have many of the same concerns, thoughts, and fears that they do.

EXERCISE A: Writing a First Draft. Choose one of the topics below. Then write a paragraph based on the prewriting information that follows. Feel free to rework the ideas that are presented below as you are writing, and do not hesitate to use some of your own ideas to assist you in developing your paragraph.

Topics:

Purposes:
Audiences:
Order:
Supporting
Information:

learning to manage your money	the rise in salaries in professional sports	negative aspects of cigarette smoking
to inform	to entertain	to persuade
young people	sports fans	your classmates
developmental	chronological	order of importance
1. keep track of all expenditures 2. keep track of all money earned and other income 3. determine regular needs and how they affect your financial situation 4. plan out a budget	1. salaries were low when professional leagues were first started 2. average salaries grew during 1960's 3. television revenues helped continue to drive salaries up 4. during the 1970's free agency caused salaries to skyrocket	1. smoking is highly addictive 2. many nonsmokers object to having to breathe in the smoke of others' cigarettes 3. there is evidence that cigarette smoke may be a health hazard for nonsmokers 4. cigarette smoking causes lung cancer, emphysema, and heart disease

EXERCISE B: More Work with First Drafts. On separate paper, write a first draft based on the prewriting activities that you completed in Exercises A and B on page 118. Do not worry about grammar, spelling, or punctuation. Just get your thoughts down on paper. Once you have finished, save your paper so that you can work on revising it.

20.3 Revising

Revising for Sense

Read your paper critically to make sure that all the ideas suport your purpose and that they are presented logically and connected clearly.

REVISING FOR SENSE
1. Make sure that you have clearly stated your topic. 2. Make sure that your main idea will be clear to your readers. 3. Make sure that there is enough supporting information. 4. Make sure that your ideas are presented in a logical order. 5. Make sure that the connections between your ideas are clear and logical.

Editing for Word Choice and Sentences

Read your paper several times, making sure that every word is the best possible one to express your thoughts and that the sentences are clear and varied.

EDITING WORDS AND SENTENCES
1. Make sure that each word means exactly what you intended it to. 2. Make sure that the language is appropriate for the intended audience. 3. Make sure that the meaning of each sentence is clear. 4. Make sure that you have varied the lengths and structures of your sentences.

Proofreading and Publishing

Proofreading involves making final corrections in spelling, capitalization, punctuation, and grammar. Once you have your final version, decide on the best way to distribute it to your intended audience.

EXERCISE A: Revising and Editing a Paper. Revise and edit the paper you wrote in Exercise B on page 119 by answering the questions below and by making appropriate changes when your response to a question is *no*.

1. Have you stated your topic clearly and made your main idea clear to your readers? _____

2. Is there enough supporting information, and is it presented in a logical manner? _____

3. Does each word in your paper convey the meaning that you intended it to? _____

4. Is the language appropriate for the intended audience, and is the meaning of each sentence clear? _____

5. Have you varied the lengths and structures of your sentences? _____

EXERCISE B: Proofreading a Paper. Proofread the paper you revised in Exercise A, correcting any errors in grammar, spelling, punctuation, and capitalization. Then recopy your paper neatly and think of how you want to present it to your audience.

21.1 Choosing Precise Words

Using Action Words

Use action verbs in the active voice to express your ideas forcefully.

Weak Verbs	Stronger Verbs
Iron gates *are* a barrier to intruders. (linking verb)	Iron gates *bar* intruders. (action verb)
The peasants *became* rebellious because of their hard lives. (linking verb)	The peasants *rebelled* because of their hard lives. (action verb)
The crowd *was impressed* by the magician. (passive voice)	The magician *impressed* the crowd. (active voice)

Using Vivid Language

Choose language that is specific and precise rather than general and dull.

General Language	Specific Language
Andy *looked* through the keyhole.	Andy *peeked* through the keyhole.
The autumn foliage was *nice*.	The autumn foliage was *brilliant*.

Choosing Words for Their Connotations

Choose the words with the most appropriate connotations for your sentences.

EXERCISE A: Using Action Verbs in the Active Voice. Rewrite each sentence, replacing the vague or imprecise verb with an action verb in the active voice.

EXAMPLE: The harsher penalty may be a deterrent to chronic offenders.
          The harsher penalty may deter chronic offenders.

1. The patient's condition became worse during the night.

   _____

2. That story has been told by Grandma for years.

   _____

3. Angie is successful at nearly everything she tries.

   _____

4. That hurricane is a threat to our area.

   _____

5. Napoleon was finally defeated by the Duke of Wellington.

   _____

EXERCISE B: Replacing General Words. On the line after each sentence, write a more exact word or expression to replace the underlined word(s).

EXAMPLE: The car came to a stop.   *screeched*

1. The artist tried out different kinds of materials. _____

2. The committee talked about the possible plans. _____

3. The World Trade Center was bigger than we expected. _____

4. The child was unhappy about the loss of his puppy. _____

5. The fireworks finale was a series of loud sounds. _____

21.2 Avoiding Worn-Out and Inappropriate Words

Avoiding Clichés

A cliché is an overused expression such as *snug as a bug in a rug*. Use precise language in place of clichés.

Clichés	Precise Expressions
Steve is *as high as a kite* about his birthday plans.	Steve is *extremely excited* about his birthday plans.
Mazie *was in a jam* because she didn't have enough money.	Mazie *had a problem* because she didn't have enough money.

Avoiding Slang

Slang is made up of words that are popular among certain groups of people at a particular time. Use precise language in place of slang words and expressions.

Slang	Precise Expressions
Jason is really *into* soccer.	Jason is really *enthusiastic about* soccer.
Gina *flipped* when she heard the news.	Gina *became excited* when she heard the news.

EXERCISE A: Eliminating Clichés. Rewrite each sentence, replacing the cliché.

EXAMPLE: Archie raced down the field like a streak of lightning.
          Archie raced down the field with amazing speed.

1. Sandy worked like a dog on that project.

   _____

2. Half the time, Bill has his head in the clouds.

   _____

3. Clutching her straight-A report card, Sue was walking on air.

   _____

4. Mom was madder than a wet hen because her car wouldn't start.

   _____

EXERCISE B: Eliminating Slang. Rewrite each sentence, replacing slang expressions with precise ones.

EXAMPLE: Most of the time Kelly seems a little loosely wrapped.
          Most of the time Kelly seems a bit disorganized.

1. My brother's table manners really gross me out.

   _____

2. My sister raps with her friends for hours on the phone.

   _____

3. If you ask me, Pat has some really flaky ideas.

   _____

4. Cal is always spacy during art class.

   _____

22.1 Expanding Short Sentences

Adding Details

Improve short sentences by adding details to the subjects, verbs, or complements.

Short Sentences	Details Added
Ellen's story won first prize.	Ellen's story, *a spooky thriller*, won first prize. (in subject)
She described both the characters and the setting.	She *vividly and realistically* described the characters and the setting. (in predicate)
I especially liked the ending.	I especially liked the *dramatic* ending. (in object)

Sentence Combining

Combine two or more short simple sentences to make a longer simple sentence, a compound sentence, a complex sentence, or a compound-complex sentence.

Short, Choppy Sentences	Combined Sentences
Ed took a shower. He fixed himself a snack. He was hot. He was hungry.	After his shower, Ed fixed himself a snack. Ed took a shower and then fixed himself a snack. Because he was hot and hungry, Ed took a shower and then fixed himself a snack.

EXERCISE A: Expanding Sentences. Add details to the sentences below.

EXAMPLE: We ordered a pizza.
             We ordered a medium pizza with pepperoni and extra cheese.

1. A teacher can inspire students.

   _____

2. Have you eaten at that restaurant?

   _____

3. The car still runs well.

   _____

4. The child looked cute.

   _____

EXERCISE B: Sentence Combining. Combine the sentences in each group below into a single sentence.

EXAMPLE: Autumn days are shorter. They are cooler too. Trees stop making chlorophyll.
             Because autumn days are shorter and cooler, trees stop making chlorophyll.

1. Monique just moved here from France. She is the new student in homeroom.

   _____

   _____

2. The model looks difficult. It is not. Follow the diagrams.

   _____

   _____

22.2 Simplifying Long, Confusing Sentences

Shortening Long Compound Sentences

Recognize compound sentences that ramble, and separate them into two or more shorter sentences.

Rambling Compound Sentence	Revision
Joe has several computer games, and Paul has several different ones, so they trade from time to time, and neither gets bored with his own.	Joe has several computer games, and Paul has several different ones. They trade from time to time, so neither gets bored with his own.

Shortening Long Complex Sentences

Recognize complex sentences that are too complicated, and separate them into shorter sentences.

Complicated Complex Sentence	Revision
The first transcontinental auto trip, which was made in 1903 when two men drove from San Francisco to New York City, was a remarkable feat because roads were poor and gasoline was hard to find.	The first transcontinental auto trip was made in 1903 when two men drove from San Francisco to New York City. It was a remarkable feat because roads were poor and gasoline was hard to find.

EXERCISE A: Shortening Long Compound Sentences. Divide each long compound sentence into two or more shorter sentences.

EXAMPLE: Few people are indifferent to cats, for most either love them or hate them, and they make no secret of their feelings.
   Few people are indifferent to cats. Most either love them or hate them and make no secret of their feelings.

1. The Nile overflowed every spring and deposited a layer of rich soil, and as a result the soil along the banks of the river never wore out.

   _____

   _____

2. Young Ben Franklin helped his father make candles and soap, but he found the work boring, and he eagerly accepted his brother's offer to teach him printing.

   _____

   _____

EXERCISE B: Shortening Complicated Complex Sentences. Divide each long complex sentence into two or more shorter sentences.

1. Although the Bisons were far behind at the half, their fans, who rarely became discouraged, continued to hope for a miracle, which occurred in the third period when the Bisons scored three quick touchdowns and held on to win.

   _____

   _____

2. The action of the movie takes place on the *Twentieth Century Limited,* a fast train which used to travel between New York and Chicago but which has been discontinued.

   _____

   _____

22.3 Using a Variety of Sentences

Using Different Sentence Openers

Begin your sentences with different openers: subjects, single-word modifiers, phrases, and clauses.

WAYS TO BEGIN SENTENCES

Subject: The *cast* and *crew* had worked very hard.
Modifier: Finally, the big night had arrived.
Phrase: Behind the curtain, the actors took their places.
Clause: As soon as the curtain rose, the audience applauded.

Using Different Sentence Structures

Use a variety of sentence structures—simple, compound, complex, and possibly compound-complex—in your writing.

Monotonous Simple Sentences	Revised with Variety
The stands were packed for the big game. The teams took the field. The fans roared. Our team had better pitching. They had better hitters. The ninth inning ended. The score was tied. The game went into extra innings.	The stands were packed for the big game. When the teams took the field, the fans roared. Our team had better pitching, but they had better hitters. When the ninth inning ended, the score was tied, so the game went into extra innings.

EXERCISE A: Using Different Sentence Openers. Rewrite each sentence to make it begin with a one-word modifier, a phrase, or a clause.

EXAMPLE: I will help you as soon as I finish my homework.
     As soon as I finish my homework, I will help you.

1. The threat of forest fires was increased because of the long drought.

   _____

2. Gerry acts quite irresponsibly sometimes.

   _____

3. Hugh entered the contest even though his chances of winning were slim.

   _____

4. A pot of geraniums sat on either side of the front steps.

   _____

EXERCISE B: Using a Variety of Sentence Structures. Rewrite the passage below using a variety of sentence structures to make it more interesting.

   Our camping trip had its share of problems from the start. Dad had reserved a site early. There were no lake-side places left. The site we did get was next to the recreation room. The sound of arcade games could be heard day and night. It didn't seem likely that we would have the peace and quiet we wanted.

_____

_____

_____

_____

_____

23.1 Recognizing Topic Sentences

The Topic Sentence in a Paragraph

The topic sentence of a paragraph presents the main idea, which all the other ideas in the paragraph support or explain.

POSITIONS FOR TOPIC SENTENCES	
Beginning	To give a sense of direction to the whole paragraph
End	To act as a summary of the whole paragraph
Middle	To give a sense of direction to the paragraph after a short introductory sentence or two

EXERCISE A: Identifying Topic Sentences. Underline the topic sentence in each paragraph below.

EXAMPLE: Although small amounts of red and yellow coloration are present in leaves throughout spring and summer, green predominates. During this time leaves are making green chlorophyll along with their food, and the green color dominates. In fall, however, as the days grow cooler and shorter, trees stop producing food and chlorophyll; and the other colors are visible. <u>Therefore, in fall, leaves don't really change color but simply reveal colors not visible before.</u>

1. Every family and every ethnic group has its own holiday customs. At Easter time, our family always has roast lamb and asparagus. The Dziubinskis have kielbasa and other sausages, while the Smiths serve baked ham. The Romanovs next door make a special breakfast bread, and the Martinos have a rice and cheese pie for dessert. Everyone, though, has brightly colored eggs.

2. Running is a form of exercise that is gaining in popularity, and with good reason. However, running has drawbacks as well as advantages. Many people find running a good way to lose weight. Others run simply to improve their cardiovascular fitness. However, many people who run on hard, paved surfaces have had back problems. Other runners have experienced pain in their feet and legs. Some sports medicine experts suggest that proper shoes can minimize the hazards of running.

EXERCISE B: More Work with Topic Sentences. Follow the directions for Exercise A.

1. My first impression was that this must be a special occasion. The entire house gleamed with the efforts of scrubbing and polishing. Fresh flowers graced the coffee table and mantel. The dining-room table glistened with silver and crystal. In addition, the aroma of sweets and spices that filled the house promised a feast to come.

2. The first step to take in getting ready to write is to find a topic of interest both to the writer and to the reader. Next the writer needs to find enough information to write clearly about the topic. A rough draft allows the writer to get the ideas on paper in a reasonable and clear order. The revision stage provides an opportunity to improve on order, sentence structure, and individual words or phrases. Taken one step at a time, writing need not be an overwhelming process.

23.2 Recognizing Supporting Information

Examples, Details, and Facts

Paragraphs may be developed with examples, details, and facts.

SOME KINDS OF SUPPORTING INFORMATION	
Examples	Specific instances of some general idea
Details	Pieces of descriptive information
Facts	Specific pieces of information that can be shown to be true

Reasons and Incidents

Paragraphs may be developed with reasons and incidents.

OTHER KINDS OF SUPPORTING INFORMATION	
Reasons	Answers that support an opinion
Incidents	Events that explain or tell a story

EXERCISE A: Examining a Paragraph. Read the following paragraph. Then answer the questions that appear below it.

(1) Home computers offer advantages to everyone in the family. (2) Recognizing this fact, software manufacturers are now packaging and promoting a wide range of programs. (3) Word-processing software encourages and simplifies correspondence and also stimulates students to improve their composition skills. (4) Budgeting and money-management programs make it possible to put the entire family budget into the computer. (5) Some programs computerize recipe files and address lists, while others provide a record of household furnishings, contents, and their value.

1. Which sentence acts as the topic sentence? _____
2. What purpose does the topic sentence serve? _____
3. Which sentences offer supporting information? _____
4. What kind of support do they present? _____
5. What is the purpose of the first sentence? _____

EXERCISE B: Deciding on Support for Topic Sentences. Read each of the following topic sentences. Then tell what kind of support you would emphasize most in each paragraph. (Use each kind of support twice.)

EXAMPLE: The Jacksons have made many improvements in the old house.
            details

1. Our vacation to the Grand Canyon was an eventful trip. _____
2. Senator Willetson deserves to be returned to the state capitol. _____
3. Street musicians add color to a city's landscape. _____
4. There are solid advantages to condominiums over single-family dwellings. _____
5. We never knew how much we depended on Gary until he moved away. _____
6. Little League should not be treated as an extension of the farm system. _____
7. Everything about the room suggested that it had been abandoned hastily. _____
8. Mom's birthday was memorable in a number of ways. _____
9. The report demonstrated that most accidents happen in the home. _____
10. Several of my classmates have found interesting ways to make money. _____

23.3 Recognizing Unity

The Unified Paragraph

A paragraph is unified if all of the ideas work together to support or develop the main idea.

ELEMENTS OF A UNIFIED PARAGRAPH
1. Main idea
2. Ideas that support or develop main idea
3. No ideas that are unrelated to the main idea

EXERCISE A: Recognizing Unity of Ideas. Decide which of the items under each topic sentence do not relate to it. Draw a line through any ideas that do not belong with the topic sentence.

EXAMPLE: Grandpa's workbench has always fascinated me.
a. jumble of jars and boxes filled with screws and nails
b. rows of paint cans and glue bottles
c. ~~the boat I made out of scrap wood~~
d. pegboard holding saws, hammers, files, and other larger tools
e. grinding wheel for sharpening blades

1. Keeping tropical fish need not be a complicated hobby.

   a. continuous filter eliminates need for cleaning tank

   b. colored gravel for added interest

   c. zebra danios as schooling fish

   d. thermostat and heater to maintain constant water temperature

   e. time-release feeder tablets for vacations

2. Although a roast turkey is part of nearly everyone's Thanksgiving dinner, the accompaniments may vary.

   a. oyster, cornbread, or herb stuffing

   b. side dishes of corn, creamed onions, cauliflower, or peas and carrots

   c. ham, rather than turkey, for Easter

   d. ethnic courses such as sausages or lasagne

   e. roast beef and Yorkshire pudding for an English Christmas

3. The April blizzard left the area paralyzed.

   a. power lines down throughout the region

   b. children happily making snowmen

   c. disabled and abandoned cars clogging roads

   d. serious accidents from skidding

   e. all schools and most businesses closed

EXERCISE B: Recognizing Unity in Paragraphs. Underline the sentences that do not support the main idea of the paragraph.

Crystals are the most orderly kind of natural matter. They are made up of atoms that occupy specific places defined by their structure. Salt crystals can be used to melt ice. This orderly arrangement of atoms is the same throughout all parts of the crystal. Crystals made from copper sulfate are blue. Despite the movement of atoms as they vibrate, they never leave their specific places in the structure.

23.4 Recognizing Coherence

Logical Orders

A coherent paragraph will follow some logical order: chronological order, spatial order, order of importance, comparison and contrast, or some other logical order suggested by the topic sentence.

LOGICAL ORDERS	
Chronological Order	Arrangement according to time sequence
Spatial Order	Presentation according to location in a scene
Order of Importance	Arrangement from least important to most important
Comparison and Contrast	Presentation of similarities or differences

Transitions

A coherent paragraph will often use transitions to help connect ideas smoothly and logically.

COMMON TRANSITIONS			
Chronological	**Spatial**	**Order of Importance**	**Comparison/Contrast**
after	above	also	also
at last	away	finally	although
before	behind	first	both
eventually	beneath	more	but
finally	inside	moreover	however
later	near	most	instead
meanwhile	next to	next	likewise
next	outside	one	similarly
then	to the right	second	whereas

EXERCISE A: Choosing a Logical Order. Each of the following items consists of a topic and supporting ideas. On the line after each topic, write which kind of order you would use to organize the supporting information in each item.

1. The scene from the top of a mountain _____
   a. the nearness to the sky   c. the vegetation on the slopes
   b. the snow on the top   d. the towns in the distance

2. Reasons for playing soccer _____
   a. getting exercise   c. making new friends
   b. learning more about the sport   d. participating in a group effort

3. A new shopping mall in town _____
   a. its appearance from the outside c. the central courtyard area
   b. the entrance   d. the kinds of shops inside

EXERCISE B: Choosing Transitions. Write at least two transitional words or phrases that you could use to help a reader follow the order you have chosen for each item in Exercise A.

1. _____

2. _____

3. _____

24.1–24.4 Writing a Paragraph

Prewriting

1. Write your topic on the line below. Make sure it's small enough for a paragraph.

TOPIC:

2. Now identify your audience. Make one up if you don't have a real one.

AUDIENCE: _____

3. Next write your main idea. What would the audience want to know?

MAIN IDEA: _____

4. Now state your purpose (to inform, persuade, describe, or narrate).

PURPOSE: _____

5. Next write your topic sentence. Try out a few before writing one below.

TOPIC SENTENCE: _____

6. On a separate piece of paper, brainstorm for support. What questions might your audience have about your topic sentence? The answers are your support.

7. Look at your page of support. Cross out any items that are not necessary. Add other support if necessary.

8. Now choose an order for your paragraph (chronological, spatial, order of importance, comparison and contrast).

ORDER: _____

9. Organize your support in the order you have chosen either by numbering the information or by preparing a modified outline on separate paper.

Writing

Using your topic sentence and organized support, write a first draft of your paragraph. Keep your audience and purpose in mind as you write. Don't worry about making everything perfect; this is only a first draft.

Revising

Write *yes* or *no* to each of the following questions. Then rework your first draft to fix all the items marked *no*.

1. Does the topic sentence clearly express the main idea of the paragraph? _____

2. Have you included enough support to develop your topic sentence? _____

3. Have you used specific supporting information rather than generalizations and weak opinions? _____

4. Is all the support necessary and related to the topic sentence? _____

5. Have you chosen the best order for your support? _____

6. Have you used transitions to help the reader understand the order? _____

7. Do you have a concluding sentence that ties your ideas together? _____

8. Is your paragraph suitable for your audience and purpose? _____

9. Are all of your sentences clear and smooth? _____

After you have improved your paragraph by turning the *no*'s into *yes*'s, **proofread** it carefully, looking for errors in grammar, mechanics, and spelling. If necessary, make a final copy and **proofread** it again.

25.1 Writing to Explain

Focusing on an Explanatory Purpose

An expository paragraph explains a factual main idea with factual, specific support that is clearly arranged for the reader.

SOME CHARACTERISTICS OF EXPOSITORY PARAGRAPHS
Topic Sentence: States a factual main idea *Support:* Strong, clear, specific factual statements

Focusing on Informative Language

The language in an expository paragraph should be informative. It should be made up of words that will help the reader understand each of the ideas you are presenting.

EXERCISE A: Planning an Expository Paragraph. Circle one of the topics below. Then complete the prewriting activities that follow.

Child-proofing a room or home   Eating for health
The best way to travel   A hard habit to break
Training a pet   Caring for house plants

1. Identify your audience. _____

2. Write a topic sentence. _____

_____

3. Write three supporting ideas. _____

_____

_____

4. Note any terms that your reader may not understand. _____

5. Tell the order you would use. _____

EXERCISE B: Writing an Expository Paragraph. Use the prewriting material above to write a short expository paragraph. Concentrate especially on clear support and specific, informative language.

_____

_____

_____

_____

_____

_____

_____

_____

_____

_____

_____

_____

25.2 Writing to Persuade

Focusing on a Persuasive Purpose

A persuasive paragraph attempts to convince a reader to accept the writer's opinion by using specific evidence that is arranged logically.

CHARACTERISTICS OF PERSUASIVE PARAGRAPHS

Topic Sentence: States a reasonable opinion on a significant topic
Support: Strong reasons, facts, and examples that attempt to
answer possible objections

Focusing on Reasonable Language

Persuasive paragraphs should use convincing but reasonable language to win readers over to the writer's viewpoint. The language should not offend anyone.

EXERCISE A: Planning a Persuasive Paragraph Circle one of the topics below. Then complete the prewriting activities that follow.

The value of vitamin supplements   The value of exercise
A maximum driving age   Hitchhiking
The value of reading the classics   Letter grades *versus* numerical grades

1. Identify your audience. _____

2. Write a topic sentence. _____

   _____

3. Write two objections that might be made by people who disagree with you.

   _____

   _____

4. List three arguments you might use. _____

   _____

   _____

5. Tell the order you would use. _____

EXERCISE B: Writing a Persuasive Paragraph. Use the prewriting material above to write a short persuasive paragraph. Concentrate on using strong support and reasonable language.

_____

_____

_____

_____

_____

_____

_____

_____

_____

_____

25.3 Writing to Describe

Focusing on a Descriptive Purpose

A descriptive paragraph creates a dominant impression of a person, place, or thing through the use of vivid details arranged so that the reader can also see or experience the thing described.

CHARACTERISTICS OF DESCRIPTIVE PARAGRAPHS
Topic Sentence: Presents a dominant impression *Support:* As many specific details as possible

Focusing on Descriptive Language

A descriptive paragraph should bring its topic to life with colorful and precise language, sensory impressions, and striking comparisons.

EXERCISE A: Planning a Descriptive Paragraph. Circle one of the topics below. Then complete the prewriting activities that follow.

A crowd of rock music fans   An ant carrying a crumb to its hill
A springtime snow storm   A street festival
A lost-and-found office   A stained-glass window

1. Identify your audience. _____

2. Write a topic sentence. _____
   _____

3. List three specific details. _____
   _____
   _____

4. List one sensory impression. _____
   _____

5. Tell the order you would use. _____

EXERCISE B: Writing a Descriptive Paragraph. Use the prewriting material above to write a short descriptive paragraph. Concentrate on using specific details; vivid, colorful language; and sensory impressions.

_____
_____
_____
_____
_____
_____
_____
_____
_____

26.1 Looking at Essays

Recognizing the Parts of an Essay

An essay has three main parts: an introduction, a body, and a conclusion. In addition, the title of an essay suggests what the essay will be about while attracting the reader's attention.

THE THREE MAIN PARTS OF AN ESSAY	
Introduction	Presents the topic in an interesting, informative way; also presents the thesis statement, expressing the main point
Body	Develops the thesis statement with specific, logically organized examples, facts, reasons, and incidents
Conclusion	Ends the essay by recalling the thesis statement and completing the writer's thoughts

Recognizing How the Parts of an Essay Work Together

The title, introduction with thesis statement, body, and conclusion of an essay must all work together to present and develop the main point for the reader's understanding and enjoyment.

EXERCISE A: Recognizing the Parts of an Essay. Carefully read the essay below. Then answer the questions that follow it.

(1) Did Mrs. O'Leary's cow really start the Chicago Fire by knocking over a lantern in the barn? Although that question will never be answered with certainty, it is certain that nature played a major role in the devastation.

(2) Throughout the summer and early fall, little rain had fallen in the region. Hot winds blowing in from the prairie made everything drier still. When fire broke out in the O'Leary barn on October 8, 1871, Chicago was like a box of kindling waiting for the touch of a match.

(3) Fierce winds spread the fire out of control in record time. In addition, they blew bits of flaming and smoldering debris onto other dry buildings. Sparks, flames, and red-hot cinders rained down throughout the night and on into Monday.

(4) Finally, late Monday night, the wind mercifully shifted and brought the rain. Whatever the cause, the devastation remained. Up to three hundred people were dead; hundreds were burned; three and a half square miles of the city lay in ashes; and more than $200 million worth of property had been destroyed.

1. What is the main point of the essay? _____

2. What is the writer's purpose? _____

3. How does the writer get the reader's attention? _____

4. In which paragraph is the thesis statement? (Underline it.) _____

5. What would be a good title for the essay? _____

EXERCISE B: More Work with Essays. Answer these questions about the essay in A above.

1. Which paragraph is the introduction? _____

2. Which paragraph is the conclusion? _____

3. What key word is used in both the introduction and the conclusion? _____

4. Which paragraphs make up the body? _____

5. What element of nature is discussed in each body paragraph? _____

26.2–26.4 Writing an Essay

Prewriting

1. Write a suitable topic on the line below. Make sure it's narrow enough.

TOPIC: _____

2. Now identify your audience, making one up if necessary. _____

AUDIENCE: _____

3. Next write the main point you want to make in your essay.

MAIN POINT: _____

4. Now state your purpose (to explain, to inform, to persuade).

PURPOSE: _____

5. Next write your thesis statement. Try out a few before writing one below.

THESIS STATEMENT: _____

6. On a separate piece of paper, brainstorm for support. What does your audience need to know? The answers are your support.

7. Look at your page of support. Identify major subtopics.

SUBTOPICS: _____

8. Choose an order for your subtopics.

ORDER: _____

9. On a separate piece of paper, make a modified outline of your essay, grouping the information under subtopics. Eliminate any unnecessary information.

10. Jot down ideas for the title, introduction, and conclusion.

Writing

Use your outline and notes to write a rough draft of your essay. Use transitions to make your thoughts flow smoothly, and keep your audience in mind as you write. Do not aim for perfection; remember this is only a first draft.

Revising

Write *yes* or *no* to each of the following questions. Then rework your first draft to fix all the items marked *no*.

1. Do you have a good title for your essay? _____

2. Is your introduction interesting and informative? _____

3. Is the thesis statement clear and appropriate to the essay? _____

4. Have you eliminated any unnecessary information? _____

5. Have you included enough examples, details, facts, reasons, or incidents to make the essay clear and interesting? _____

6. Have you used the best and clearest order for the subtopics? _____

7. Have you used enough transitions to make the essay read smoothly? _____

8. Does the conclusion tie the essay together by referring to the main point? _____

After you have improved your paragraph by turning the *no*'s into *yes*'s, **proofread** carefully, looking for errors in grammar, mechanics, and spelling. If necessary, make a final copy and **proofread** it again.

27.1 Looking at Reports

Sources of Information

A report should include footnotes giving credit to all outside sources. At the end of a report a bibliography should list all the sources that were used in the preparation and writing of the report.

Sample Footnote	Sample Bibliography Entry
[1]John Gunther, <u>Julius Caesar</u>, p. 63.	Gunther, John. <u>Julius Caesar</u>. New York: Random House, 1959.

The Basic Structure of a Report

A report is a unified paper on a single topic, based on information gathered from research. It has a title, an introduction with a thesis statement, a body, a conclusion, footnotes, and a bibliography.

EXERCISE A: Working with Sources of Information. Choose one of the topics listed below. Use the library card catalog and *The Readers' Guide* to write footnote and bibliography entries for the kinds of sources described below.

Cape Cod	Migration of geese
O. Henry	Volcanoes
Hunting dogs	J. S. Bach

EXAMPLE: Footnote for a signed encyclopedia article

    1   Encyclopedia Americana,   1970 ed., "Volcano," by L. Don Leet

1. Footnote for a book by one or more authors

   _____

2. Bibliography entry for a book by one author

   _____

3. Bibliography entry for a book by two or more authors

   _____

4. Footnote for a signed magazine article

   _____

5. Bibliography entry for a magazine article (either signed or unsigned)

   _____

EXERCISE B: Understanding the Parts of a Report. Use what you have learned about reports to answer these questions.

1. Where is the thesis statement usually found? _____

2. What is the purpose of the body of the report? _____

3. What is the purpose of footnotes? _____

4. What is a bibliography and where is it usually found? _____

   _____

5. What should a conclusion do? _____

27.2 Writing a Report

Prewriting

1. Select a topic that is interesting, that can be supported with enough information, and that is narrow enough. Write it below.

TOPIC: _____

2. On file cards, list complete information about each source you plan to use.

3. On a separate sheet of paper, write 3–5 questions that you plan to answer.

4. On the same paper, write a rough draft of your thesis statement.

5. On note cards, take careful notes to answer the questions you asked about your topic. Remember to include page references on each card.

6. When you have finished your research, decide on a logical order for your report.

ORDER: _____

7. On separate paper, make a modified outline of your report.

8. Organize your note cards to follow your outline.

Writing

Use your outline and note cards to write a first draft of your report with footnotes and a bibliography. Use transitions to link your ideas throughout the report. Don't try to make everything perfect, since this is just a rough draft. Do, however, number and keep track of footnotes.

Revising

Write *yes* or *no* to each of the following questions. Then rework your first draft to fix all the items marked *no*.

1. Do you have an interesting title? _____

2. Do you have an interesting introduction with a clear thesis statement? _____

3. Do the body paragraphs develop the thesis statement? _____

4. Do transitions clearly link your ideas throughout the report? _____

5. Does the conclusion summarize the main point of the report? _____

6. Does your report include footnotes from at least three different sources? _____

7. Are all quotations, borrowed ideas, and little-known facts clearly credited? _____

8. Do your footnotes follow the appropriate form? _____

9. Are all sources listed correctly in the bibliography? _____

10. Is your bibliography in alphabetical order? _____

After you have improved your report by turning the *no*'s into *yes*'s, **proofread** carefully, looking for errors in grammar, mechanics, and spelling. If necessary, make a final copy and **proofread** it again.

WRITING PROCESS PAGE

28.1 Looking at Book Reports

The Format of a Book Report

One particularly useful format for a book report has the three parts shown in the chart.

PARTS OF A BOOK REPORT	
Introduction	Identifies the book by title and author and gives a brief summary of the contents
Body	Focuses on specific elements of the book, such as theme, character, plot, or setting
Conclusion	Gives an overall evaluation of the book and makes a recommendation

EXERCISE A: Understanding a Book Report. Carefully read the book report below. Then complete the activities that follow.

(1) *Treasure Island,* the classic novel by Robert Louis Stevenson, is a fast-paced adventure tale of pirates and their quest for gold. The reader is immediately drawn into the excitement as the tale is told by the young Jim Hawkins, who is at the center of the action.

(2) The conflict centers on the struggle to possess a treasure map that Jim found in the sea chest of old Billy Bones and gave to his friends Squire Trelawney and Dr. Livesey. The map in hand, the squire outfits the schooner *Hispanola* to sail in search of the treasure, little knowing that many of the sailors in his crew are unscrupulous pirates. Their leader, the peg-legged Long John Silver, plans a mutiny to capture both the ship and the treasure map. There then follows a series of land and shipboard battles, plots, and scheming until the conflict is finally resolved.

(3) The carefully drawn characters heighten the conflict and excitement of the novel. The noble Dr. Livesey and the eccentric Ben Gunn, the sole inhabitant of the island, are central to the plot's resolution. The menacing Long John Silver and his ruthless pirate friends move the action forward and make the conflict more intense.

1. What two elements of the novel does the writer examine?

   (a) _____   (b) _____

2. What important characters does the writer mention? _____

   _____

3. What kind of order is used in paragraph 2? _____

4. Underline the transitional words and expressions that make the order clear.

EXERCISE B: Writing a Conclusion. Write a conclusion for the book report above. Be sure it draws together the information in the report. Give a favorable evaluation and recommendation.

_____

_____

_____

_____

_____

28.2 Writing a Book Report

Prewriting

1. Choose a book that you have read recently. Identify it in the spaces below.

TITLE: _____

AUTHOR: _____

2. Decide which elements of the book you want to focus on.

ELEMENTS: _____

3. On a separate piece of paper, write a short summary of the book.

4. On the same piece of paper, list specific information—examples, details, incidents, and statements by the author or characters—to support the elements you chose in #2.

5. Decide on a logical order for organizing your support.

ORDER: _____

6. Use a modified outline to group your support according to the elements and order you have chosen.

Writing

Using your modified outline, write a first draft of your book report. The first paragraph should include enough information about the book so that the report will make sense to someone who has not read the book. Then discuss the elements you have chosen, and end with an evaluation.

Revising

Write *yes* or *no* to each of the following questions. Then rework your first draft to fix all the items marked *no*.

1. Does your introduction identify the book by title and author? _____

2. Does the introduction include a brief summary of the book? _____

3. Have you included enough information to make your ideas clear? _____

4. Have you eliminated any unnecessary information? _____

5. Have you included the best possible examples? _____

6. If you have used quotations, are they accurate? _____ Have you included page references in parentheses? _____

7. Have you used enough transitions to make the book report read smoothly? _____

8. Are your introduction and conclusion clear and interesting? _____

After you have improved your book report by turning the *no's* into *yes's*, **proofread** carefully, looking for errors in grammar, mechanics, and spelling. If necessary, make a final copy and **proofread** it again.

WRITING PROCESS PAGE

29.1 Journals

Understanding Journals

A journal is an ongoing record of important experiences, events, and personal observations.

KINDS OF JOURNALS	
Purposes of Journals	**Probable Writing Time**
To summarize everyday experiences	Daily
To express personal feelings and insights	Daily or several times a week
To record important events	Several times a week
To record experiences in an area of special interest	As each occasion arises

Keeping a Journal

Record ideas, events, and impressions in chronological order, and include clear and memorable details.

EXERCISE A: Understanding the Purpose of Journal Entries. Read each item below and determine the purpose the writer probably had in writing it.

EXAMPLE: Becoming an aunt was a real thrill. _To record an important event_

1. When I caught my first touchdown pass yesterday, I felt as though all my extra practice had finally paid off. _____

2. Today was very dull and boring. _____

3. I really want to ask Marcia out, but every time I talk to her I start stuttering and my palms get sweaty. _____

4. I like going places with Chuck, but he gets mad when I do anything with somebody else. _____

5. It's true! My father has accepted a job as a game show host, and we are moving to Los Angeles. _____

EXERCISE B: Planning a Journal Entry. Choose one of the topics below or a topic of your own. Then answer the questions to plan a journal entry.

A new experience   A family crisis
A funny coincidence   A victory

1. When? _____

2. Who? _____

3. Where? _____

4. What? _____

_____

_____

5. Your reactions? _____

_____

_____

_____

_____

_____

_____

29.2 Autobiographies

Understanding Autobiographies

An autobiography is a writer's account of his or her life.

FEATURES OF AN AUTOBIOGRAPHY	
1. First-person point of view	4. Characters
2. Setting	5. Dialogue
3. Incidents arranged in chronological order	6. Descriptive details

EXERCISE A: Understanding an Autobiography. Carefully read the selection below. Then answer the questions that follow it.

My autograph collection consists of a single specimen acquired at the first symphony concert I ever attended when I was in seventh grade. The Minneapolis Symphony, led by Eugene Ormandy, was appearing at a local movie theater. This was not one of the box-like cinemas that spring up around today's shopping malls but a lavish picture palace from the 20's, with long velvet curtains that parted to reveal the screen and an ornate chandelier that was lighted mainly for Bank Night drawings.

During the first half of the program, I reveled in the surges of sound from the strings and the shouts from the brass. Then at intermission a school friend mentioned that he planned to get Ormandy's autograph after the performance. Unwilling to let any part of this great experience slip away, I resolved to get my program autographed also. Alas, this decision ruined the rest of the concert for me, for I dreaded the prospect of approaching this famous man.

I delayed going backstage, and as a result I fell far behind the other autograph-seekers. I got lost in the unfamiliar maze of dusty dressing rooms and store rooms and the tangle of weights and pulleys backstage. When I reached the room the orchestra had occupied below stage, it was almost empty. Ormandy had been whisked off to a reception. Most of the musicians had already boarded their bus. One balding, middle-aged man was putting a cello into its case. Adjusting my expectations to reality, I promptly requested his autograph. Gravely he wrote, "Best Regards, Sam Reiner, first cello."

It's my only autograph, but I prize it. In later years, I always looked for Reiner when I attended symphony concerts and was always glad to see him sawing away, gravely and competently.

1. What is the time span of this selection? _____

2. What event does the writer describe? _____

3. How old was the writer when it occurred? _____

4. What other characters appear in this episode? _____

5. What is the general setting of the selection? _____

EXERCISE B: More Work with Autobiographies. Answer these questions about the selection above.

1. What specific setting does the writer describe in the first paragraph? What details make it vivid? ____
_____

2. What details are given about the setting in the third paragraph? _____
_____

3. How do the writer's feelings change during the second paragraph? _____

4. What one element from the chart above does the writer *not* use? Why is the selection effective without it? _____

5. The incident turns out differently from what the reader and writer originally expected. How does the writer feel about the outcome? _____

29.2 Writing an Autobiography

Prewriting

1. First choose the time span your autobiography will cover.

TIME SPAN: _____

2. Then identify the setting.

SETTING: _____

3. Give some descriptive details about the setting.

DETAILS: _____

4. Next, decide what incidents you will include.

INCIDENTS: _____

_____

5. Now, list the characters involved in these incidents.

CHARACTERS: _____

_____

6. Give some descriptive details about the characters.

DETAILS: _____

_____

7. Number the incidents in chronological order.

Writing

Use your notes to write a first draft of your autobiography. Follow chronological order, and use transitions, descriptive details, and dialogue to help your readers follow the events. Don't aim for perfection. This is only a first draft, and you will have a chance to improve it.

Revising

Write *yes* or *no* to answer each of the following questions. Then rework your first draft to fix all the items marked *no*.

1. Have you used the first-person point of view throughout? _____
2. Is the time span clearly defined? _____
3. Is the setting made clear to the reader? _____
4. Do the events follow in chronological order? _____
5. Have you used vivid descriptive details? _____
6. Have you included personal observations or feelings? _____

After you have improved your autobiography by turning all the *no*'s into *yes*'s, **proofread** carefully, looking for errors in grammar, mechanics, and spelling. If necessary, make a final copy and **proofread** it again.

30.1 Writing a Character Sketch

Recognizing the Basic Features of a Character Sketch

A character sketch should focus on a dominant impression of a person.

ELEMENTS OF A CHARACTER SKETCH	
Beginning	Establishes a strong, definite direction by giving a dominant impression of the person
Middle	Development of the impression through lively details of physical description, actions, and words
Ending	A strong concluding idea, perhaps illustrated by a "telling" final detail to make the character memorable
Language	Lively, exact, and vivid

EXERCISE A: Recognizing Elements of a Character Sketch. Read the partial character sketch below. Then answer the questions that follow it.

In stature, behavior, and personality, Ms. MacDougal is perfectly suited to her job. On the playground, she can easily be mistaken for an older child supervising the kindergarteners. She bounds about with her charges, taking part in their games of tag and dodge ball, and most fifth-graders tower over her.

Ms. MacDougal's classroom exhibits her boundless enthusiasm and encourages the children's own. Her colorful cartoon drawings playfully teach shapes, numbers, and colors. At sharing time, she sits on the rug with the children and examines, plays with, and exclaims over each new toy produced by her eager charges. Her hazel eyes dance with her own enthusiasm and the children's eagerness.

1. What physical details does the writer mention? _____

2. What actions suggest Ms. MacDougal's character? _____

_____

3. What is the dominant impression you have? _____

4. What kinds of material support that impression? _____

5. List three specific verbs that suggest Ms. MacDougal's liveliness.

_____

EXERCISE B: Developing a Dominant Impression. Make up an incident that could be used to illustrate the dominant impression in the partial character sketch above. Try to use exact, vivid language.

_____

_____

_____

_____

_____

_____

_____

_____

_____

_____

30.1 Writing a Character Sketch

Prewriting

1. Choose a real or imaginary character to write about.

CHARACTER: _____

2. Identify an outstanding characteristic of the person and write it below.

CHARACTERISTIC: _____

3. Next write one or two sentences to introduce the character and express a dominant impression. Try out a few before writing below.

INTRODUCTION/DOMINANT IMPRESSION: _____

_____

_____

4. On a separate piece of paper, list physical details, incidents, and other information that will develop the dominant impression.

5. Decide on a logical order that will help your information support the dominant impression.

ORDER: _____

6. Work with your page of supporting information. Eliminate weak items, and arrange the details in the order you have chosen.

Writing

Use your prewriting material to write a rough draft of your character sketch. Don't aim for perfection since this is only a first draft.

Revising

Write *yes* or *no* to each of the following questions. Then rework your first draft to fix all the items marked *no*.

1. Does your opening sentence establish a sharp impression of the person? _____

2. Have you used enough details to support the impression? _____

3. Have you chosen the best order to make the details clear and interesting to your reader? _____

4. Have you chosen vivid words to bring your subject to life? _____

5. Have you chosen the best way to close your sketch? _____

After you have improved your character sketch by turning the *no*'s into *yes*'s, **proofread** carefully, looking for errors in grammar, mechanics, and spelling. If necessary, make a final copy and **proofread** it again.

30.2 Writing a Short Short Story

Recognizing the Basic Features of a Short Story

A short short story should describe characters and setting clearly, present and resolve a conflict, be told from a consistent point of view, follow a chronological order, and include dialogue where appropriate.

FEATURES OF A SHORT SHORT STORY	
Characters	The people involved in the story
Setting	The time and place where the story takes place
Conflict	A problem to be resolved or obstacle to be overcome
Chronological Order	Showing the action as it unfolds
Dialogue	Exact words spoken by a character; conversation between characters

POINTS OF VIEW	
First-person Narrator	The storyteller writes as a character in the story to whom the story is happening.
Third-person Narrator	The storyteller does not take part in the story but is able to tell characters' thoughts as well as actions.

EXERCISE A: Recognizing Features of a Short Short Story. Identify each item below as (1) character, (2) setting, (3) conflict, or (4) dialogue. Then identify the narrator as (a) first person or (b) third person.

EXAMPLE: I wondered how we would ever escape.   ___3, a___

1. Sue was thinking jealously of Janice's high test scores. _____

2. We lay on the beach enjoying the warmth of the sun and the distant cries of sea gulls. _____

3. "Meet me in the library," Tom whispered to me. _____

4. Ben's mind was racing. "How can I ever get to Joe in time?" he wondered. _____

5. The two dashed through the summer downpour toward the bandstand. _____

EXERCISE B: Examining a Short Short Story. Find a short short story in a book or magazine. Then answer the following questions.

1. Who are the characters? _____

2. What is the time of the setting? _____

3. What is the place of the setting? _____

4. What is the main conflict? _____

5. What point of view is used? _____

W
R
I
T
I
N
G

P
R
O
C
E
S
S

P
A
G
E

30.2 Writing a Short Short Story

Prewriting

1. List two or more characters who are central to your story.

CHARACTERS: _____

2. Next describe the time and place of the setting.

SETTING: _____

3. Now describe the central conflict of the story.

CONFLICT: _____

4. Write the point of view from which the story will be told.

POINT OF VIEW: _____

5. On a separate piece of paper, write in chronological order the events of the story.

6. On the same piece of paper, list your characters and record specific details that will make them come to life.

7. On your list of events, mark places where dialogue will make the story more lively or will help move the action forward.

Writing

Use the prewriting activities above to write a first draft. Maintain a consistent point of view and make your characters act, talk, and think to resolve the conflict. Don't try to make everything perfect; just try to move the story along. This is only your first draft, and you will have a chance to improve it.

Revising

Write *yes* or *no* to each of the following questions. Then rework your first draft to fix all the items marked *no*.

1. Are your characters described clearly enough for your readers to see them as you do? _____

2. Is your setting clearly described? _____

3. Have you presented and resolved some interesting conflict or problem? _____

4. Have you kept a consistent point of view throughout the story? _____

5. Have you used dialogue to make the story interesting and realistic? _____

6. Will your ending leave the reader satisfied? _____

After you have improved your short short story by turning the *no*'s into *yes*'s, **proofread** carefully, looking for errors in grammar, mechanics, and spelling. If necessary, make a final copy and **proofread** it again.

31.1 Looking at Friendly Letters, Social Notes, and Business Letters

Setting Up Friendly Letters and Social Notes

A friendly letter or social note should include a heading, a salutation, a body, a closing, and a signature. To write the basic parts of a friendly letter or social note, use either the indented style or the semiblock style. On the envelope, include your full return address and a complete mailing address, using the same style you used in the letter, either indented or semiblock.

THE PARTS OF FRIENDLY LETTERS AND SOCIAL NOTES	
Heading	Your address and the date
Salutation	The greeting (Dear _____,)
Body	Any information you want to send
Closing	A slightly formal, casual, or affectionate sign-off
Signature	Your name

STYLES FOR FRIENDLY LETTERS AND SOCIAL NOTES	
Indented	Heading, closing, and signature are not lined up vertically.
Semiblock	Heading, closing, and signature are lined up vertically.

EXERCISE A: Working with the Parts of Friendly Letters. Follow the instructions below.

1. Write two headings, the first in indented style and the second in semiblock style.

_____   _____

_____   _____

_____   _____

2. Write two salutations.

_____   _____

3. Write two closings and signatures, the first in indented style and the second in semiblock style.

_____   _____

_____   _____

4. Which parts of a friendly letter begin on the right? _____

5. Which parts begin on the left? _____

EXERCISE B: Addressing an Envelope. In the space below, address an envelope in semiblock style.

```



```

31.1 Looking at Friendly Letters, Social Notes, and Business Letters

Setting Up Business Letters

A business letter should include a heading, an inside address, a salutation, a body, a closing, and a signature. To write the basic parts of a business letter, use either the block style or the semiblock style. On a business envelope, you should include your full return address and a mailing address that matches the inside address of the letter exactly.

THE PARTS OF A BUSINESS LETTER	
Heading	Your address and the date
Inside Address	The name and sometimes the title of the recipient and the address of the person or business
Salutation	The greeting (Dear _____:)
Body	The message or informtion
Closing	A formal sign-off
Signature	Your name, written in ink

EXERCISE A: Working with the Parts of Business Letters. Follow the instructions below.

1. Write two inside addresses.

_____   _____
_____   _____
_____   _____
_____   _____

2. Write two salutations.

_____   _____

3. In which style does everything begin on the left? _____

4. What should be the main feature of the body? _____

5. What should go at the top of the second page, if any? _____
_____

EXERCISE B: Addressing a Business Envelope. In the space below, address an envelope for one of the inside addresses you wrote in A, above.

31.2 Writing Different Kinds of Letters

Writing Friendly Letters and Social Notes

The purpose of a friendly letter is to share news as well as your thoughts and feelings. Learn the characteristics of social notes, such as invitations, letters of acceptance and regret, and thank-you notes.

KINDS OF SOCIAL NOTES	
Invitation	Occasion, date, time, place, information about what to bring or wear; R.S.V.P.
Letter of Acceptance	Repetition of date, time, and place; appreciation for having been invited.
Letter of Regret	Prompt, definite explanation for being unable to attend; gratitude for having been invited.
Thank-you Note	Expression of gratitude for thoughtfulness; prompt and explicit mention of the gift or occasion.

Writing Business Letters

Learn the characteristics and purposes of a number of different kinds of business letters.

KINDS OF BUSINESS LETTERS	
Request	Polite request for information or material.
Order	Item name, quantity, price, size, and other specifics; dollar amount of order and payment method; source from which you are ordering; date needed.
Complaint	Polite request to adjust an order or correct a mistake; information to aid in resolution of problem.
Opinion	Praise or criticism of some action; expression of opinion, clear statement of opinion with support.

EXERCISE A: Writing Friendly Letters and Social Notes. On a separate piece of paper, write a letter for one of the following purposes.

To accept or decline an invitation
To thank your aunt for a gift
To congratulate a friend for an award

To tell a friend who is away at camp about local news

EXERCISE B: Writing a Business Letter. Again on a separate piece of paper, write one of these business letters.

To question the amount of a bill
To order tickets for a concert

To express your opinion on a local issue
To complain about a damaged mail-order item

32.1 Preparing Answers to Essay Exams

Understanding the Question

Plan your time for essay examinations and pace yourself to make sure you stay on schedule. Read each question carefully to see exactly what information it asks for.

KEY WORDS IN ESSAY EXAM QUESTIONS	
Key Words	**What You Should Do**
Compare	Look for and explain likenesses.
Contrast	Look for and explain differences.
Define	Tell what something is; use examples.
Describe	Give features, details, and organization.
Diagram	Make a drawing or chart, label and explain it.
Discuss	Give facts and examples to support a general statement.
Explain	Give information that tells why, what, and how.
In your opinion	State your opinion and support it.

Planning Your Answer

When you understand the question, you are ready to plan an answer. Plan your answer by listing your ideas in a modified outline.

EXERCISE A: Understanding the Question. Underline the key word or words in each essay question below. Then tell what you would do to answer the question.

EXAMPLE: <u>Discuss</u> the role of pre-election polls in presidential elections.
         Give facts and examples to support a general statement.

1. Contrast the role of women in today's work force with the role of women in the work force fifty years ago. _____

    _____

2. Discuss the importance of education. _____

    _____

3. Explain how longitude and latitude provide a good way of locating a point on the earth's surface.

    _____

4. In your opinion, how has the development of rock videos affected the music industry? _____

    _____

5. Describe a typical crowd at a professional football game. _____

    _____

EXERCISE B: Planning an Answer. Choose one of the essay questions from Exercise A. Then in the space provided below arrange the main idea and major details in modified outline form.

Main Idea _____

    _____

Major Details   1. _____

        2. _____

        3. _____

        4. _____

        5. _____

32.1 Preparing Answers to Essay Exams

Writing Your Answer

Let your modified outline guide you as you start writing your answer to the question.

Checking Your Answer

Check your answers before handing in your examination. Proofread your paper, checking for accuracy.

CHECKING YOUR ANSWER

1. Make sure that you answered the question directly and clearly.
2. Make sure that you included a clear topic sentence or thesis statement.
3. Make sure that you included enough supporting information.
4. Make sure that you used correct grammar, spelling, and mechanics.

EXERCISE A: Answering an Essay Question. Using the outline you prepared in Exercise B on page 150, write a one-paragraph answer in the space provided below.

_____

_____

_____

_____

_____

_____

_____

_____

_____

_____

_____

_____

_____

_____

_____

_____

EXERCISE B: Checking Your Answer. Check the answer you wrote in Exercise A by answering the questions below. If your response to any of the questions is *no*, make the appropriate changes to improve your paper.

1. Did you answer the question clearly and directly? _____
2. Did you include a clear topic sentence? _____
3. Did you include enough supporting information? _____
4. Did you use correct grammar and mechanics? _____
5. Are all the words in your answer spelled correctly? _____

33.1 Ways to Enlarge Your Vocabulary

Setting Up a Vocabulary Notebook

Set up a vocabulary notebook and use a dictionary to add new words to your vocabulary. Use "bridge" words to help you remember definitions.

SETTING UP A NOTEBOOK PAGE		
Word	**Bridge**	**Definition**
crustacean	crust	a sea animal with a hard shell

Using Other Study Methods

Use a variety of methods for studying and reviewing new words.

STUDY METHODS
1. Set up three-column vocabulary pages by subject area in your notebook. 2. Use index cards to make vocabulary flash cards. 3. Use a tape recorder to review definitions and uses of words. 4. Work with a partner, taking turns quizzing each other on new words.

EXERCISE A: Working with the Three-Column Notebook Method. Complete the chart below, using a dictionary to supply missing definitions. Make up your own bridge words—those that will help *you* remember the meanings. Study the new words and their meanings.

EXAMPLE: ferocious ___*lion*___   ___*extremely savage; fierce*___

Word   Bridge   Definition

1. gratuity   _____   _____
2. distraught   _____   _____
3. germinate   _____   _____
4. spontaneous   _____   _____
5. tremulous   _____   _____
6. falsetto   _____   _____
7. conifer   _____   _____
8. recapitulate   _____   _____
9. vacillate   _____   _____
10. intractible   _____   _____

EXERCISE B: Using Other Study Methods. Use a dictionary to look up the definition of each word below, and write the definition in the space provided. Copy each word on one side of an index card. On the other side copy its definition. Work with a partner, quizzing each other on the definitions.

EXAMPLE: portage   ___*the carrying of boats and supplies overland between two waterways*___

Word   Definition

1. reprimand   _____
2. spelunker   _____
3. derogatory   _____
4. disgruntled   _____
5. mandatory   _____

33.2 Using Context

Using Context in Daily Reading

Use context clues to guess the meanings of unfamiliar words.

STEPS IN USING CONTEXT CLUES

1. Reread the sentence, leaving out the unfamiliar word.
2. Examine the surrounding words to see if they give any clues.
3. Use the clues to guess the meaning of the word.
4. Read the sentence again, substituting your guess to see if it makes sense.
5. Check your guess by looking up the word in a dictionary.
6. Write the word and the definition in your vocabulary notebook.

Using Context in Science

Use context clues to guess the meanings of technical words or words with special meanings.

Using Context in Social Studies

Use context clues to guess the meanings of difficult words or words used in special ways.

EXERCISE A: Using Context in Daily Reading. Read the passage below. Circle the correct meaning of each underlined word.

And now, as I still continued to step cautiously onward, there came (1) <u>thronging</u> upon my recollection a thousand vague rumors of Toledo. Of the dungeons there had been strange things (2) <u>narrated</u>—fables I had always deemed them,—but yet strange, and too ghastly to repeat, (3) <u>save</u> in a whisper. Was I left to (4) <u>perish</u> of starvation in this (5) <u>subterranean</u> world of darkness; or what fate, perhaps even more fearful, awaited me?—Edgar Allan Poe, "The Pit and the Pendulum"

EXAMPLE: recollection (a) assortment (b) memory (c) mind (d) fear

1. thronging (a) pounding (b) throbbing (c) aching (d) crowding
2. narrated (a) sold (b) told (c) promised (d) happened
3. save (a) rescue (b) keep (c) except (d) dangerous
4. perish (a) die (b) flourish (c) hunger (d) survive
5. subterranean (a) above ground (b) underwater (c) underground (d) scary

EXERCISE B: More Work with Context Clues. Write a definition for each underlined word. Then check your definitions in a dictionary.

EXAMPLE: Both pines and hemlocks are <u>coniferous</u> trees. ___cone-bearing___

1. Because it is officially a <u>neutral</u> country, Switzerland has never been involved in a war. _____

2. Napoleon's army was <u>vanquished</u> at the Battle of Waterloo. _____

3. Because of the fluid in his lungs, the patient's <u>respiration</u> was labored. _____

4. In contrast to chemically active gases, neon is <u>inert</u>. _____

5. In fall, geese <u>migrate</u> to warmer, southern regions; in spring they return to their native northern homes. _____

33.3 Using Structure

Using Prefixes

An easy way to enlarge your vocabulary is to learn the meanings of a few common prefixes. Notice that some prefixes change their spelling when they combine with certain words or roots.

TEN COMMON PREFIXES			
ad- (ac-, ap-, as-)	to, toward	post-	after
com- (co-, con-, cor-)	with, together	re-	back, again
dis-	away, apart	sub- (suc-, suf-, sup-)	beneath, under
ex-	from, out	trans-	across
mis-	wrong	un-	not

EXERCISE A: Using Prefixes to Define Words. Write a brief definition of each of the words below. Check your definition in a dictionary.

EXAMPLE: accumulate _____*to gather together*_____

1. disassemble _____

2. transcontinental _____

3. acknowledge _____

4. suppress _____

5. undesirable _____

6. misunderstanding _____

7. rearrange _____

8. correspond _____

9. postoperative _____

10. excavate _____

EXERCISE B: Using Prefixes to Write Words. Use each prefix below (or one of its other spellings) to compose a word. Then write the definition of the word. Check your definition in a dictionary.

EXAMPLE: sub- _____*subway*_____   _____*underground railway*_____

1. ad- _____   _____

2. com- _____   _____

3. dis- _____   _____

4. ex- _____   _____

5. mis- _____   _____

6. post- _____   _____

7. re- _____   _____

8. sub- _____   _____

9. trans- _____   _____

10. un- _____   _____

33.3 Using Structure

Using Roots

The root carries the basic meanings of the word. Notice that each of these roots has more than one spelling. A variant spelling for each root is shown in parentheses.

TEN COMMON ROOTS		
-cap- (-capt-) take, seize	-spec- (-spect-)	see
-dic- (-dict-) say or point out	-ten- (-tain-)	hold
-mit- (-mis-) send	-ven- (-vent-)	come
-mov- (-mot-) move	-vert- (-vers-)	turn
-pon- (-pos-) put, place	-vid- (-vis-)	see

EXERCISE A: Using Roots to Define Words. Match the words in the first column with the meanings in the second. Place the correct number next to the meaning.

1. retain   _____ any of several parts that may be put together

2. motion   _____ act or result of turning toward

3. component   _____ look back over

4. dismiss   _____ a coming toward

5. advent   _____ one who looks into things; investigator

6. capture   _____ act or state of moving

7. revision   _____ hold back

8. conversion   _____ that which is said to another to write down

9. inspector   _____ send away

10. dictation   _____ the act or result of seizing

EXERCISE B: Using Roots to Compose Words. Use each of the roots below (or its variant spelling) to compose a word. Define each word and use a dictionary to check your definition.

EXAMPLE: -pon-   _repository_   _a place where things are put for safekeeping_

1. -cap-   _____   _____

2. -dic-   _____   _____

3. -mit-   _____   _____

4. -mov-   _____   _____

5. -pon-   _____   _____

6. -spec- _____   _____

7. -ten-   _____   _____

8. -ven-   _____   _____

9. -vert- _____   _____

10. -vid- _____   _____

33.3 Using Structure

Using Suffixes

A suffix is one or more syllables added at the end of a root to form a new word. A suffix usually changes the word's part of speech.

SEVEN COMMON SUFFIXES			
-able (-ible)	capable of being	-ly	in a certain way
-ance (-ence)	the act of	-ment	the result of being
-ful	full of	-tion (-ion,	the act of or state of
-ity	the state of being	-sion)	being

EXERCISE A: Using Suffixes to Define Words. Match the words in the first column with the meanings in the second. Place the correct number next to the meaning.

1. prediction   _____ capable of being noticed

2. merciful   _____ act of relying on

3. announcement   _____ capable of being divided

4. noticeable   _____ a foretelling

5. creativity   _____ the result of being announced

6. reluctantly   _____ act or state of being sent

7. reliance   _____ act of being dependent

8. divisible   _____ full of mercy

9. mission   _____ in a reluctant way

10. dependence   _____ state of being creative

EXERCISE B: More Work with Suffixes. Define each word below. Use the meaning of the suffix in writing the definition.

EXAMPLE: lovable   _capable of being loved_

1. permanence _____

2. security _____

3. creation _____

4. admissible _____

5. entertainment _____

6. sorrowful _____

7. luxuriance _____

8. remarkable _____

9. surprisingly _____

10. contradiction _____

33.4 Exploring Word Origins

Loanwords

Loanwords are words in the English language that have been borrowed from other languages.

Old Words with New Meanings

The English language grows by giving new meanings to existing words and by combining existing words in new ways.

Coinages

The English language grows through the addition of newly coined words.

KINDS OF COINAGES	
Acronyms: UNICEF	*Blends:* telecast
Clipped Words: sub	*Brand Names:* Calvin's
"People" Words: guillotine	

EXERCISE A: Finding the Sources of Borrowed Words. Look up each word below in a dictionary and write the language of origin. If more than one language is given, write the one listed first.

EXAMPLE: chauffeur   _French_

1. tomato _____
2. poncho _____
3. pasta _____
4. portage _____
5. noodle _____
6. sheik _____
7. cauldron _____
8. raccoon _____
9. typhoon _____
10. pretzel _____

EXERCISE B: More Work with Word Origins. Label each word below as a *combination, acronym, clipped word, "people" word, blend,* or *brand name.* Then write either the words from which it is formed or the identity of the person or product it is taken from.

EXAMPLE: twiddle   _blend, twirl + fiddle_

1. begonia _____
2. footnote _____
3. Ping-Pong _____
4. smog _____
5. mike _____
6. AWOL _____
7. frizzle _____
8. mesmerize _____
9. uke _____
10. Velcro _____

34.1 Solving Your Spelling Problems

Your Personal Spelling List

Make a list of words that you misspell, write the list in your notebook, and review it regularly.

PERSONAL SPELLING LIST FORMAT			
Word	**Pronunciation**	**Definition**	**Sentence/Memory Aid**
solem*n*	so*l′* m	serious	In solem*n*ize the *n* is pronounced.
station*ery*	stā′ sh n r ē	writing paper	Use station*ery* to write *letters*.

A System for Improving Your Spelling

Use the following method to study the words on your personal spelling list.

A METHOD FOR LEARNING PROBLEM WORDS
1. *Look* at each word and notice the arrangement of letters.
2. *Pronounce* the word, syllable by syllable.
3. *Write* the word. Say each syllable aloud as you write it.
4. *Compare* the word you wrote with the word in your notebook. If you misspelled the word, circle the incorrect letters and repeat the method.

EXERCISE A: Working with Problem Words. In the following sentences, circle the correctly spelled word in parentheses. Use a dictionary to check your answers. Record any errors in your spelling notebook.

EXAMPLE: The ((defendant,) defendent) pleaded not guilty.

1. We planned a (surprise, surprize) party for Paul.
2. Our class is having an (amature, amateur) talent night.
3. Mom was (suspicious, suspicius) of our explanation.
4. The two houses look quite (simalar, similar) from the outside.
5. Voting is a duty as well as a (priviledge, privilege).
6. Jamie is an exceptional (athelete, athlete).
7. We eat in the dining room only on special (ocassions, occasions).
8. A good commander will never (desert, dessert) his troops.
9. Did you ask Mrs. Warner for her chili (recipie, recipe)?
10. The pianist gave an (extraordinary, extrordinary) performance.

EXERCISE B: Spelling Problem Words. Correct the spelling of each of these misspelled words. Use a dictionary to check your answers.

EXAMPLE: royelty _____*royalty*_____

1. calander _____
2. rehersed _____
3. outragous _____
4. obvius _____
5. enviroment _____
6. mathamatics _____
7. illistration _____
8. lisence _____
9. nutral _____
10. protene _____

34.1 Solving Your Spelling Problems

Developing Memory Aids

Use memory aids to help you remember the spelling of words that are difficult for you.

PLAN FOR USING MEMORY AIDS
1. Associate letters in the word with letters in related words.
2. Look for short, easy-to-spell words within the difficult word.

Studying Common Spelling Demons

Study the words on a list of spelling demons to find out which ones you need to work on.

EXERCISE A: Developing Memory Aids. Write a memory aid of your own for each word listed below. Circle the difficult part of the word and the important part of your memory aid.

EXAMPLES: calendar _____calendar—end of the month_____
capitol _____capitol—dome_____

1. extraordinary _____

2. believe _____

3. dessert _____

4. principal _____

5. separate _____

6. thorough _____

7. committee _____

8. behavior _____

9. nuisance _____

10. courageous _____

EXERCISE B: Finding Misspelled Demons. Each line contains one misspelled demon. Write it correctly in the space provided.

EXAMPLE: barrel   desparate   misspell   _____desperate_____

1. anniversary   exercise   opinnion   _____

2. aukward   deceive   rehearse   _____

3. familier   eighth   lawyer   _____

4. captain   knowledge   spaggetti   _____

5. naturally   restarant   curious   _____

6. paralell   disappoint   prairie   _____

7. whether   succede   condemn   _____

8. preperation   envelope   aisle   _____

9. rhythm   foreign   labratory   _____

10. library   abcense   straight   _____

34.2 Following Spelling Rules

Forming Plurals

A regular plural is one that is formed by adding either -s or -es to the singular form of the noun. Use your dictionary to check the correct spelling of words with irregular plurals.

SAMPLE PLURALS			
Singular	**Plural**	**Singular**	**Plural**
chestnut	chestnuts	piano	pianos
class	classes	lady-in-waiting	ladies-in-waiting
rose bush	rose bushes	sheriff	sheriffs
bench	benches	cloverleaf	cloverleaves
tomato	tomatoes	pulley	pulleys
henchman	henchmen	child	children
crisis	crises	goose	geese
datum	data	sheep	sheep

Most compound nouns written as single words form their plurals regularly. Compound nouns written with hyphens or as separate words generally form the plural by making the modified word plural.

EXERCISE A: Writing Plurals. Write the plural of each word below in the space provided.

EXAMPLE: strawberry _____strawberries_____

1. belief _____
2. jury _____
3. brother-in-law _____
4. moose _____
5. wharf _____
6. portfolio _____
7. ditch _____
8. tax _____
9. library _____
10. bus _____

11. analysis _____
12. stereo _____
13. man-at-arms _____
14. sweet potato _____
15. patch _____
16. monkey _____
17. self _____
18. reindeer _____
19. mouse _____
20. matchbox _____

EXERCISE B: More Work with Plurals. In each blank, fill in the correct plural form of the word in parentheses.

EXAMPLE: The three ___alarm clocks___ went off at different times. (alarm clock)

1. *Cagney and Lacey* is a show about _____. (policewoman)
2. The rancher branded each of the _____. (calf)
3. _____ are more serious crimes than misdemeanors. (felony)
4. The forecast calls for _____ throughout the day. (snow flurry)
5. This jelly was made from _____. (gooseberry)
6. _____ sometimes set off unnecessary information. (parenthesis)
7. Both of those _____ carry cars, as well as passengers. (ferry boat)
8. Several large _____ blew down during the storm. (branch)
9. _____ are sometimes called "pigskins." (football)
10. The farmer hitched a team of _____ to the wagon. (ox)

34.2 Following Spelling Rules

Adding Prefixes

When a prefix is added to a root or root word, the spelling of the root stays the same.

ADDING PREFIXES	
dis- + service = disservice	re- + examine = reexamine
mis- + spell = misspell	un- + natural = unnatural

Adding Suffixes

Be aware of spelling changes needed in some root words when a suffix is added.

ADDING SUFFIXES	
harm + -ed = harmed	move + -able = movable
deny + -ing = denying	recur + -ing = recurring
manage + -able = manageable	deny + -ed = denied
grace + -ful = graceful	happy + -ly = happily

EXERCISE A: Spelling Words with Prefixes. Form new words by combining one of the prefixes below with each of the numbered roots.

dis- mis- re- un-

EXAMPLE: appear ___disappear___

1. necessary _____
2. management _____
3. trust _____
4. noticed _____
5. spent _____
6. friendly _____
7. satisfied _____
8. direct _____
9. regard _____
10. involved _____
11. spoken _____
12. evaluate _____
13. unified _____
14. imaginative _____
15. consider _____
16. tasteful _____
17. establish _____
18. named _____
19. stated _____
20. respect _____

EXERCISE B: Spelling Words with Suffixes. Write the new word formed by combining each of the following words and suffixes.

EXAMPLE: commit + -ed ___committed___

1. bounty + -ful _____
2. refer + -ing _____
3. trap + -ed _____
4. entertain + -ment _____
5. deter + -ence _____
6. outrage + -ous _____
7. wonderful + -ly _____
8. grab + -ed _____
9. handy + -ly _____
10. concur + ence _____
11. acquit + -ed _____
12. foresee + -able _____
13. brag + -ing _____
14. encourage + -ing _____
15. argue + -ment _____
16. permit + -ing _____
17. merry + -ly _____
18. compare + -able _____
19. observe + -ance _____
20. suffer + -ing _____

34.2 Following Spelling Rules

Deciding on *ie* or *ei*

When a word has a long *e* sound, use *ie*. When a word has a long *a* sound, use *ei*. When a word has a long *e* sound but is preceded by the letter *c*, use *ei*.

COMMON *ie* AND *ei* WORDS			
Long e Sound	**Long a Sound**	**Long e After c**	**Exceptions**
grief	neighbor	deceive	either
niece	rein	ceiling	neither
thief	weigh	receive	seize

Using *-cede*, *-ceed*, and *-sede*

Memorize the words that end in *-cede*, *-ceed*, and *-sede*.

-cede Words		*-sede* Word	*-ceed* Words
concede	recede	supersede	proceed
intercede	secede		exceed
precede			succeed

EXERCISE A: Spelling Words with *ie* and *ei*. Fill in the blank in each sentence with the correctly spelled word in parentheses.

EXAMPLE: The child ___*grieved*___ over the loss of his puppy.   (greived, grieved)

1. The treasure was buried in a corn _____.   (feild, field)

2. That dog is a golden _____.   (retreiver, retriever)

3. Mom immediately _____ that something was wrong.   (perceived, percieved)

4. The movie begins at _____ o'clock.   (eight, ieght)

5. Sue asked for another _____ of cake.   (peice, piece)

6. Tom and Beth brought _____ records.   (their, thier)

7. We cannot get a rebate without the _____.   (receipt, reciept)

8. Ed's athletic _____ are remarkable.   (acheivements, achievements)

9. The _____ of the building surprised us.   (height, hieght)

10. A team of horses pulled the _____.   (sleigh, sliegh)

EXERCISE B: Spelling Words with *-cede*, *-sede*, and *-ceed*. On the line at the right, write the correctly spelled word in each group.

EXAMPLE: recede, resede, receed ___*recede*___

1. seceding, seseding, seceeding _____

2. excedingly, exsedingly, exceedingly _____

3. cede, sede, ceed _____

4. procedes, prosedes, proceeds _____

5. precede, presede, preceed _____

6. supercede, supersede, superceed _____

7. succede, sucsede, succeed _____

8. accede, acsede, acceed _____

9. interceded, interseded, interseeded _____

10. antecedent, antesedent, anteceedent _____

35.1 Establishing Good Study Habits

Choosing a Study Setting

Establish a study area that works well for you.

Scheduling Study Time

Establish a regular study schedule and follow it each night.

```
┌─────────────────────────────────────────────────────────┐
│              HINTS FOR SCHEDULING STUDY TIME              │
│                                                           │
│   1. Plan to study during the hours when you are most alert. │
│   2. Plan to study in blocks of time about a half-hour each. │
│   3. Plan to study your most difficult subjects first each night. │
│   4. Plan to follow the same schedule Monday through Thursday. │
│   5. Plan to complete short-term projects before continuing with │
│      long-term ones.                                      │
│   6. Set aside a special time for pleasure reading each day. │
│   7. Post your study schedule in a visible place as a daily reminder. │
└─────────────────────────────────────────────────────────┘
```

Keeping Track of Assignments

Use an assignment book to record homework assignments and due dates.

EXERCISE A: Making a Weekly Study Schedule. In the space below, make a study schedule for the week. Use thirty-minute blocks of time. Start by blocking in all the activities that are already part of your day, such as an after-school activity.

Time	Monday	Tuesday	Wednesday	Thursday	Friday

EXERCISE B: Using an Assignment Book. Keep track of work assigned to you in each of your classes in the space provided below for one week. Then set up an assignment section like the one below in your notebook or in a separate assignment book.

Date	Subject	Assignment	Due	Finished

35.2 Developing Your Note-Taking Skills

Keeping an Organized Notebook

Keep a neat, well-organized, and complete notebook.

Making Modified Outlines

Use a modified outline for recording notes briefly and quickly.

Making Formal Outlines

Use a formal outline to group detailed information precisely according to main ideas, major details, minor details, and subdetails.

RULES FOR MAKING FORMAL OUTLINES

1. Every level must have at least two items: An outline must have a I and a II; an A must have a B; a 1 must have a 2; and so on.
2. Every new level of detail should be indented.
3. All Roman numerals should be in line, all capital letters in line, all regular numbers in line, and all small letters in line.
4. The first word in each item should be capitalized.
5. A period should be placed after each number or letter.

Writing Summaries

Use a summary to record information in a shortened form.

RULES FOR WRITING SUMMARIES

1. Identify important words and main ideas as you hear or read them.
2. Hold the main ideas in your mind or jot them down.
3. Combine important information into general statements.
4. Express these statements in your own words, using complete sentences.

EXERCISE A: Using Outlines. Select a section of the chapter you are currently studying in social studies. On a separate piece of paper, write a modified outline or a formal outline of that section, whichever your teacher prefers.

EXERCISE B: Writing a Summary. Select a newspaper or magazine article that interests you. Use the questions below to plan a summary of the article.

1. What is the title of the article and who wrote it? _____

2. Where and when was the article published? _____

3. What is the main idea of the article? _____

4. What are the supporting ideas? _____

_____

5. Write the main idea and supporting details in summary form.

_____

_____

_____

_____

_____

36.1 Forms of Reasoning

Using Fact and Opinion

Analyze your material to determine whether or not it is based on reliable information.

QUESTIONS TO ASK TO TELL FACTS FROM OPINIONS
1. Can the statement of fact be checked to *verify*, or prove, that it is true? How?
2. If the statement cannot be verified as a fact, it is an opinion. Are there supporting facts to make the opinion *valid*?

Using Inference and Generalization

Think logically to draw valid conclusions.

FORMS OF REASONING		
Form	Valid Use	Invalid Use
Inference	A reasonable conclusion based on the information being examined	An interpretation or statement that does not follow from the information being examined
Generalization	A conclusion that is based on a large number of examples and takes any exceptions or qualifying factors into account	A conclusion that is based on too few examples or ignores exceptions or qualifying factors

EXERCISE A: Distinguishing Between Fact and Opinion. Identify each of the statements below as a *fact* or an *opinion*.

EXAMPLE: The average man is taller than the average woman.   *opinion*

1. The Edmonton Oilers won the Stanley Cup in 1985. _____

2. The Edmonton Oilers were the best hockey team in the world in 1985. _____

3. The weather in Florida is much nicer than the weather in Maine. _____

4. Florida has a warmer climate than Maine does. _____

5. The United States has the most democratic form of government of any country in the world. _____

EXERCISE B: Analyzing Forms of Reasoning. Identify the form of reasoning used in each of the following statements as *inference* or *generalization*. Then determine whether each of the conclusions drawn is valid or invalid.

EXAMPLE: Jim is very intelligent and works very hard in school, so he must be a good student.
   inference   *valid*

1. My three sisters always do well in English class. Therefore, all girls do well in English class. _____ _____

2. Allison is a good bowler, and she plays the piano well, so she must be a talented artist. _____ _____

3. Last year, there were thousands of alcohol-related traffic fatalities. Therefore, it is very dangerous for anyone to drink and drive. _____ _____

4. Ron is a gifted athlete, and he has been skiing since he was two years old, so he must be a good skier. _____ _____

5. All basketball players are poor students. _____ _____

36.2 Language and Thinking

Uses of Language

Learn to identify different uses of language.

USES OF LANGUAGE	
Denotation	Words used to present facts or describe a situation objectively
Connotation	Words used to imply a particular point of view and convey a positive or negative attitude
Jargon	The use of words with specialized meanings in a particular trade or profession

EXERCISE A: Analyzing the Uses of Language. Identify each of the items below as *denotation, connotation,* or *jargon.*

EXAMPLE: Sally drove from New York to Vermont.   *denotation*

1. The scientists hypothesized for several hours in an attempt to ascertain the significance of the experiment. _____

2. Lucy's lazy husband lay on the couch snoring while she struggled to make the house presentable for the guest they were expecting. _____

3. Juan walked slowly down the road. _____

4. Pete ate three hamburgers and two frankfurters for lunch. _____

5. Mr. Jackson's dull and boring speech lasted for two hours. _____

6. At the beginning of each semester, Mrs. Manishevitz takes inventory of her students' interests. _____

7. Jack spent New Year's Day watching football games on television. _____

8. Susan wasted the afternoon watching cartoons on television. _____

9. Students at Webster High School are placed in classes according to their proficiency-achievement levels. _____

10. Raymond studied all night for his biology test. _____

EXERCISE B: More Work with the Uses of Language. Follow the directions in Exercise A.

1. The doctor determined that the disease is caused by ultramicroscopic infective agents. _____

2. A mean-looking man dresssed in black lurked outside of the doorway. _____

3. A man stood against the wall by the front door. _____

4. Chico cooked roast beef, carrots, cabbage, and potatoes for his family. _____

5. Rhonda unselfishly agreed to relieve her mother of the burden of cooking dinner for a night. _____

NAME _____ CLASS _____ DATE _____

37.1 Developing Your Reading Skills

Examining Textbooks

Identify and make use of the special sections at the front and back of your textbooks.

PARTS OF TEXTBOOKS
Table of Contents: (front) List of units and chapters and the pages on which they begin
Preface: (front) Statement of the author's purpose and sometimes an explanation of special features
Index: (back) Alphabetical list of topics covered and the pages on which they appear
Glossary: (back) Alphabetical list of difficult or specialized terms and their definitions
Appendix: (back) Charts, lists, documents, essays, or other material the author considers useful to the reader
Bibliography: (back) Books the author has used in writing the book and possibly other interesting books related to the subject

Using Textbooks to Study

Use the organization of your textbooks to help you study them effectively.

EXERCISE A: Using the Parts of Textbooks. Write the part of a textbook in which you would look first to find each kind of information.

EXAMPLE: A list of Presidents and Vice-Presidents   *appendix*

1. The number of chapters in Unit III _____

2. The page on which the term *laissez-faire* is introduced _____

3. An explanation of special features in the book _____

4. The meaning of the word *proletariat* _____

5. The number of pages in Chapter 18 _____

6. Maps showing the the growth of the British Empire _____

7. The title and author of a related book on the Industrial Revolution _____

8. The page on which the chapter about the Industrial Revolution begins _____

9. The page(s) on which capitalism is discussed _____

10. The author's reason for writing the book _____

EXERCISE B: Using a Textbook to Study. Choose a chapter in one of your textbooks to use in completing the work below.

1. List the chapter headings and subheadings. _____

2. Turn two of these headings into questions. _____

3. Read the chapter. Then answer the questions you wrote in #2. _____

4. What are the main ideas contained in the chapter? _____

5. List the major details used to support one of these ideas. _____

Copyright © by Prentice-Hall, Inc.

167

37.1 Developing Your Reading Skills

Using Different Reading Styles

Learn to choose the style of reading suitable to your purpose and material.

DIFFERENT READING STYLES		
Style	**Definition**	**Use**
Phrase Reading	Reading groups of words in order to understand all material	For studying, solving problems, and following directions
Skimming	Skipping words in order to read rapidly and get a quick overview	For previewing, reviewing, and locating information
Scanning	Reading in order to locate a particular piece of information	For researching, reviewing, and finding information

Reading Critically

Read critically in order to question, analyze, and evaluate what you read.

CRITICAL-READING SKILLS
1. Understanding the difference between statements of *fact* and *opinion*
2. Making *inferences* from material presented to come to a conclusion about the main idea in writing
3. Recognizing the *tone* the author uses in writing and noticing how it gives clues to the author's purpose
4. Recognizing any *persuasive techniques* used and what effects they have

EXERCISE A: Determining Which Reading Style to Use. Determine which of the reading styles referred to in the chart above would be most appropriate for each of the purposes below.

EXAMPLE: Finding a specific section in a reference book ___*scanning*___

1. Reviewing a chapter of a novel for a class discussion _____

2. Reading a section of a science book in order to answer the questions at the end of a

chapter _____

3. Locating a quote to use in a book report _____

4. Previewing a section of a textbook that a teacher is going to be lecturing on the next

day _____

5. Reading a section of a textbook for the first time _____

EXERCISE B: Applying Critical-Reading Skills. Find a newspaper or magazine article that interests you. Then answer the questions below, using the article as your source.

1. Find two statements of fact in the article. _____

_____

2. What sources could you use to verify the statements of fact you wrote in #1? _____

_____

3. Find two statements of opinion in the article. _____

_____

4. Are the statements of opinion you wrote in #3 validated in the article? If so, how? _____

_____

5. What inferences or conclusions did you draw about the main idea or ideas in the article? _____

_____

37.2 Taking Tests

Preparing for Tests

Schedule time for several days before a test in order to prepare for it.

PREPARING FOR TESTS

1. Find out about the nature of the test and what sorts of questions will be on it.
2. Review any class or reading notes that relate to the material you are going to be tested on.
3. Check your knowledge by making up questions on the material you will be tested on.
4. Memorize material by going over it repeatedly for several days before the test.

Taking Objective Tests

Budget your time among looking over the test, answering the questions, and proofreading.

PROOFREADING YOUR ANSWERS

1. Check to see that your name is on each sheet of paper.
2. Make sure that you have followed directions accurately and completely and that you have answered all the questions.
3. Read all the test questions and your answers. Correct any errors and add any answers you were not sure of before.

EXERCISE A: Preparing for a Test. Answer the questions below.

1. How can you make sure that you will have enough time to review and memorize all the material you need to know for the test? _____
_____

2. Why is a test not a true measurement of your knowledge when you cram for it at the last minute?
_____

3. How can you determine which areas you should devote extra study time to? _____
_____

4. Why is it important to go over material repeatedly for several days before a test? _____
_____

5. Give an example of a way in which you and a friend can assist one another in studying for a test.
_____

EXERCISE B: Taking Objective Tests. Answer the questions below.

1. What items should you bring to a test with you? _____
_____

2. Why is it important to arrive at a test on time or early? _____
_____

3. What should you be aware of when you first skim through a test? _____
_____

4. What types of questions should you plan to devote the most time to? _____
_____

5. What is the first step you should take in proofreading a test? _____
_____

38.1 Using the Library

The Card Catalog

Use the card catalog to find a book by author, title, or subject. Consult catalog cards to find publishing information, a description of features, related subject headings, and the location symbol for each book. Use word-by-word alphabetizing and a few additional rules to find cards in the catalog.

Finding Books on the Shelves

In most libraries, fiction, nonfiction, and biographies are arranged in different ways. Reference books and young adult books may be grouped separately.

Fiction	Arranged in alphabetical order by author's last name
Nonfiction	Arranged by call numbers based on the Dewey Decimal System of Classification
Biography	Arranged in alphabetical order by subject's last name

EXERCISE A: Finding Information from Catalog Cards. Use information on the catalog cards below to answer the questions that follow.

1.
```
VOLCANOES

551.2  Gribbin, John
G      This shaking earth by John Gribbin,
       Putnam, 1978
       191 p. ill.
```

2.
```
Hertz, Louis Heilbrouer

629.1331  The complete book of model
          aircraft, spacecraft, and rockets by
          Louis Heilbrouer Hertz, Crown
          Publishers 1967.
          x. 278 p. ill., ports. 27cm
          bibliog. p. 269
```

1. Who is the author of the book about model aircraft? _____

2. What is the title of the book published by Putnam? _____

3. Which book contains a bibliography? _____

4. Which card is the author card? _____

5. What kind of card is the other card? _____

EXERCISE B: Finding Books in the Library. Complete the following activities.

1. Number the following fiction books in the order in which you would find them on the shelves.

    _____ a. *The Scarlet Letter* by Nathaniel Hawthorne

    _____ b. *The Marble Faun* by Nathaniel Hawthorne

    _____ c. *The Sound and the Fury* by William Faulkner

    _____ d. *Ethan Frome* by Edith Wharton

    _____ e. *So Big* by Edna Ferber

2. Number these biographical works in the order in which they are found on the shelves.

    _____ a. *Langston Hughes: Poet of His People* by Elisabeth P. Myers

    _____ b. *Abe Lincoln Grows Up* by Carl Sandburg

    _____ c. *Daniel Boone* by James Daugherty

    _____ d. *Of Courage Undaunted: Across the Continent with Lewis and Clark* by James Daugherty

    _____ e. *Jules Verne: Portrait of a Prophet* by Russell Freedman

38.2 Finding Reference Books in the Library

General Reference Books

Use encyclopedias for basic facts, background information, and bibliographies. Use almanacs to find a number of different kinds of miscellaneous information. Use atlases to find information from maps.

Specialized Reference Books

Use specialized dictionaries to find detailed information about words. Use specialized encyclopedias to find detailed information on a topic. Use biographical reference books to find information about people.

Periodicals

Use magazines and journals to find concise, current information. Use *The Readers' Guide to Periodical Literature* to find information in magazines and journals.

LOOKING UP THE INFORMATION IN *THE READERS' GUIDE*

1. Begin with the most recent issue of *The Readers' Guide.*
2. Look up the subject you are interested in. Subjects are listed alphabetically.
3. Read the list of articles for your subject and choose those you want to see.
4. Copy the names, volume numbers, dates, and page numbers of the magazines you want; check the key in the front if necessary.
5. Give your list to the librarian, who will get the magazines for you.

EXERCISE A: Recognizing Uses of Reference Books. Match each item in the first column with the reference book in which it can be found.

a. General information about Lebanon   _____ 1. an atlas

b. Three synonyms for *esoteric*   _____ 2. an encyclopedia

c. Lakes in Minnesota   _____ 3. *Current Biography*

d. Information about Geraldine Ferarro   _____ 4. *Composers Since 1900*

e. Two paintings by Grandma Moses   _____ 5. *Modern Men of Science*

f. Three novels by Hawthorne   _____ 6. *The World Almanac*

g. Music by Cole Porter   _____ 7. *American Authors 1600–1900*

h. Information about Einstein   _____ 8. *Roget's Pocket Thesaurus*

i. The population of Dayton, Ohio   _____ 9. *Peoples of the Earth*

j. Marriage customs of the Maori   _____10. *Notable American Women*

EXERCISE B: Using *The Readers' Guide*. In the library, look up one of the following subjects in *The Readers' Guide*. Then answer the questions below.

Subjects: Word Processing, Grammy Awards, the Super Bowl, Acid Rain, Skiing

1. What is the date on *The Readers' Guide* that you used? _____

2. What subheadings of the topic does the listing have? _____

3. What, if any, cross-references to other subjects are given? _____

4. What is the title of one article listed under your subject? _____

5. What is the name of the magazine, volume number, date, and page numbers of the article you listed in #4? _____

38.3 Using the Dictionary

A Dictionary for Everyday Use

Use a dictionary that best suits your present needs.

Using Your Dictionary to Check Spelling

Become familiar with the different spelling patterns of the sounds of English words.

Finding Words Quickly

Learn to use alphabetical order quickly to find words in the dictionary.

STEPS FOR FINDING WORDS QUICKLY
1. Use the Four-Section Approach. 2. Next use the guide words. 3. Then follow strict, letter-by-letter alphabetical order.

Understanding Main Entries

Learn to recognize and use the different kinds of information contained in a main entry.

COMMON INFORMATION IN MAIN ENTRIES			
spelling	part-of-speech labels	special labels	derived words
syllabification	etymologies	idioms	synonyms
pronunciation	definitions		

EXERCISE A: Finding Words Quickly to Check Spelling. For each word write the section (1, 2, 3, or 4) in which you would look for it, the guide words on the page on which you find it, and its phonetic spelling.

EXAMPLE:	Section	Guide Words	Phonetic Spelling
cholera	1	choir/chop suey	kol′ ər ə
1. guitar	_____	_____	_____
2. wretched	_____	_____	_____
3. cinnamon	_____	_____	_____
4. rhinoceros	_____	_____	_____
5. psychic	_____	_____	_____

EXERCISE B: Using the Dictionary. Use a dictionary to answer the following questions.

1. What is an anemone? _____

2. What is the meaning of the idiom *with a grain of salt*? _____

3. What are three synonyms for *nimble*? _____

4. What is the plural of *criterion*? _____

5. What is the noun form of *droll*? _____

6. What other forms are given for the prefix *in-*? _____

7. What is the etymology of *buckaroo*? _____

8. Divide *practitioner* into syllables. _____

9. What is the usual spelling of *flavour*? _____

10. What does the acronym BASIC stand for? _____

39.1 Informal Speaking Skills

Speaking in Class Discussions

Develop confidence about participating in class through preparation and practice.

TAKING PART IN CLASSROOM DISCUSSIONS
1. Set goals for your participation. 2. Do extra reading on the topic you are studying. 3. Plan what you might say prior to the discussion. 4. Raise your hand and volunteer to contribute. 5. Follow the discussion carefully. 6. Observe methods used by others.

Giving Directions

When giving directions, be as clear and accurate in your language as possible. Do not confuse your listeners by using vague, overly general statements.

Making Introductions

Before introducing a person, find out, write down, and memorize all pertinent information about that person.

Making Announcements

When making an announcement, supply answers to the questions *who? what? when? why?* and *how?*

EXERCISE A: Preparing for a Classroom Discussion. Prepare for an upcoming classroom discussion by answering the questions below.

1. What goals have you set for your participation? _____
_____
_____

2. What extra reading could you do so that you will have something of special interest to say? _____
_____

3. What points might you be able to make? _____
_____
_____

4. How should you go about contributing to the discussion? _____

5. How will you know when it is a good time for you to contribute? _____
_____

EXERCISE B: Preparing to Make an Announcement. Prepare to make an announcement about a real or imaginary event by answering the questions below.

1. Whom does the announcement concern? _____
2. What is the event being announced? _____
3. Where is the event taking place? _____
4. When is it taking place? _____
5. Why is the announcement being made? _____

39.2 Formal Speaking Skills

Recognizing Different Kinds of Speeches

Choose the kind of speech you will give by considering both the purpose of the speech and your audience.

KINDS OF SPEECHES	
Expository	Given to explain an idea, a process, or an object
Persuasive	Given to try to get the listener to agree with the speaker's position
Entertaining	Given to offer the listeners something to enjoy

Planning Your Speech

Choose a subject that you know or like in order to interest your audience. Then outline your speech and prepare note cards to assist you when you deliver your speech.

PLANNING A SPEECH
Choose a topic. Gather necessary information. Organize the information into an outline. Prepare note cards.

EXERCISE A: Identifying Kinds of Speeches. Label each of the following speech topics as *expository,* *persuasive,* or *entertaining.*

EXAMPLE: Why the school year should be lengthened   _persuasive_

1. How to be a better football player _____

2. Mountain climbing _____

3. The animals of Africa _____

4. The need for gun control _____

5. The music of the sixties _____

6. How to maintain your own automobile _____

7. The need for more parking space in a small town _____

8. Why prison sentences should be longer _____

9. How to defend yourself against an attacker _____

10. Sky diving _____

EXERCISE B: Choosing a Topic. Choose a speech topic that will interest each type of audience listed below.

EXAMPLE: Striking workers   _Why a new contract proposal should be accepted_

1. Actors _____

2. Young children _____

3. Musicians _____

4. Sports fans _____

5. Doctors _____

6. Lawyers _____

7. Tax payers _____

8. Historians _____

9. Teachers _____

10. Artists _____

39.2 Formal Speaking Skills

Delivering Your Speech
Practice your speech to gain confidence.

DELIVERING A SPEECH

1. Do not read to your audience.
2. Pronounce your words clearly.
3. Be aware of nonverbal language, such as your movements, posture, facial expressions, and gestures, while you practice delivering your speech.
4. Stay within the time limit you were given for your speech.
5. Be prepared to answer questions from your audience.

Evaluating a Speech

Evaluate a speech in a way that offers benefits both to the speaker and to yourself.

ITEMS TO CONSIDER WHEN EVALUATING A SPEECH

1. Type of speech
2. Clarity and development
3. Use of details to support main ideas
4. Use of unspoken language
5. Voice projection

EXERCISE A: Delivering a Speech. Answer the questions below.

1. Why is it important to practice your speech before delivering it? _____
_____

2. What is nonverbal language? _____
_____

3. How often should you refer to your note cards? _____

4. What determines how long your speech should be? _____

5. What should you be prepared to do after you have finished delivering your speech? _____
_____

EXERCISE B: Evaluating a Speech. Evaluate a speech given in class by answering the questions below.

1. What type of speech was given? _____

2. Did the speaker introduce the topic clearly and develop it well? Support your answer. _____
_____

3. Did the speaker support main ideas with appropriate details? Give two examples. _____
_____

4. Was the speaker's voice loud enough? _____

5. Did the speaker appear confident and support his or her verbal delivery with appropriate nonverbal language? Support your answer. _____
_____

39.3 Listening Skills

Preparing to Listen

Prepare to listen by giving the speaker your complete attention.

SUGGESTIONS FOR PREPARING TO LISTEN

1. Start with a positive attitude.
2. Focus your eyes and ears on the speaker.
3. Concentrate on what the speaker is saying.
4. Block out any distractions.
5. Put away anything that may detract from your paying attention to the speaker.
6. Keep a pencil and paper handy in case you want to take notes.
7. Try to find out in advance what topic will be discussed.

Selecting Information to Remember

Identify and remember the main points and major details while you are listening to the speaker.

IDENTIFYING MAIN IDEAS AND MAJOR DETAILS

1. What is the general topic?
2. What important points are being made about the topic?
3. What needs to be remembered about each point?
4. What examples or facts relate to each point?
5. What clues is the speaker giving about something's importance?
6. Does the speaker repeat an idea or phrase a number of times?
7. What is written on the blackboard?

EXERCISE A: Preparing Yourself to Listen. Answer the questions below.

1. What is the difference between hearing and listening? _____

_____

2. How can you avoid daydreaming? _____

_____

3. Why should you have a pencil and paper with you when someone speaks? _____

_____

4. Why is it helpful to find out in advance what topic will be discussed? _____

_____

5. How can your physical condition affect your ability to pay attention? _____

_____

EXERCISE B: Listening for Main Ideas and Major Details. Work on improving your listening skills by writing down the main ideas and major details of a lecture given in one of your classes. Use the spaces provided below.

1. Main idea _____

2. Major detail _____

3. Major detail _____

4. Major detail _____

5. Major detail _____